Custom Bike Building Basics

CHRIS CALLEN

Published by:
Wolfgang Publications Inc.
P.O. Box 223
Stillwater, MN 55082
www.wolfpub.com

First published in 2012 by Wolfgang Publications Inc.,
P.O. Box 223, Stillwater MN 55082

ISBN 10: 1-935828-62-2
ISBN 13: 978-1-935828-62-4

Printed and bound in U.S.A.

Custom Bike Building Basics

Page 21

Page 99

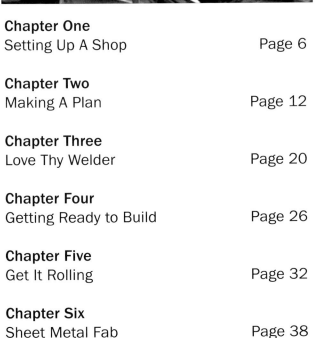

Introduction

So why would the staff of a national motorcycle magazine get together on a book about the basics of custom motorcycle building? The answer is simple enough: it had to be done. With so much of what is happening in the custom world today being centered around the garage builder, much like it was in the seventies, more people are looking for information to "Do It Your Self" than ever before. It's a combination of a tough economy, a younger generation with fewer resources and last but not least, the inner fire that compels each age group to do it different, their way.

While there are scores of television shows and manuscripts to show the average Joe what products are available and the high end procedures of accomplished fabricators who make them and build the incredible bikes of today, there are almost none who tell you how to get from dreaming of a custom bike to the point of working with your hands. That's where this book comes in. What we humbly intend to do is give you the basic foundation of what it takes to build a truly custom motorcycle. This book will not give you a list of parts or builders to contact for work. Instead it will indoctrinate you with the theory and practices that we believe should be taught at the basic level.

In these pages we will take you from the first steps of setting up your workspace, through making a plan, forming relationships, understanding metals and tools, all the way through cutting your first perfectly good part in half to make it better. Join the staff of Cycle Source Magazine as they retrace their roots and unveil the honest truth about chopping for the love of it. As you are guided through the chapters, Paul Wideman, Roadside Marty, Chad Lemme, Darren McKeag and editor, Chris Callen will explain why they do what they do and help you to pick the right path to begin a lifetime of customizing for yourself.

Acknowledgements

I have to tell you the truth, when Tim Remus came to us to write a book on behalf of the *Cycle Source* magazine, I was a little unsure about how we would go about it. Fortunately for us he was tolerant to our somewhat unconventional behavior and let us come up with our own recipe for what we felt would be a good book for the times. You see, we know a ton of the current top builders, some are on our very own staff, but where we felt the industry is going today is another step backwards to the roots of garage building. I can remember my own days coming up around the garage we called Pappy's shack in the early eighties. I'm not sure if it was my young age or just those times but it wasn't at all comfortable to just go around asking questions so the process of learning to build bikes came slowly. Let's face it, no one wants to ask a stupid question, no matter how receptive the audience.

What we hope to accomplish with *Custom Bike Building Basics* is to set a foundation to help the reader gain confidence and a vocabulary to go out and get those questions answered. With the new direction of the industry, or more importantly the resurgence of the home mechanic, this is the perfect time for a book like this. This could have never been possible without the help and guidance of so many people and we would like to just take a few minutes and thank them all publicly.

First and foremost we want to thank Paughco. The second build you will follow in this book is one almost entirely made from Paughco parts with the help of Jason, who spent countless hours helping us get the right stuff, and Ron Paugh himself who made it all possible.

To Roadside Marty and his father Shelton Davis who took me in like a stray and taught me the old ways of building the Panhead. Without Roadside, none of this would have been possible. Thanks for helping me make a 1949 dream come true. Bobby and Elisa Seeger from Indian Larry Motorcycles for killer Indian Larry forward controls, as well as my assembly crew: Matt Reel, Zach Williams, Duke Miller, Keith Parson, and Daniel Donley from Pandemonium. There's also the St. Louis late night crew: Russ, Chad Lemme and Darren McKeag. Very special thanks to Chris Gatto at Cycle Parts Warehouse for helping with the quick and most bitchin' NOS parts. Lincoln Electric for the tools to get the job done. None of this would have got off the ground without Joel Jansen and his crew at Handy Lifts who made sure we had the best working environment. James Gaskets who never let us down. Fabricator Kevin for being a true mentor and helping Roadside make the "Chick Magnet" an icon in our time.

I couldn't do a list of thanks without mentioning some of the guys from Limpnickie Lot. Thanks to Tim Anding at Papa Clutch who made me the deal of a lifetime on the Panhead motor to begin with, what a perfect set of '49 cases. Also some big props to Jeremy Pedersen from Relic Custom Stripes who put the most killer flake job on a bike that has ever been done in the history of hippy, trippy, freak paint.

Special thanks to my main help at the Source Garage, Robbie Keller and his old man, my brother Rob. To my brother and lifelong mentor, Albert Moore, who is a great example and has always provided us with inspiration and good advice. He also did the chrome on "Ticket To Ride" and it was a big honor to have his influence. Ron Tonetti and Sara Liberte from North Hills Cycle, for reminding me that I am not a professional mechanic.

We would be ashamed if we didn't put a special thanks in to Old Man Dave who taught so many of us what it meant to be a biker and why we should put the damn tools back where they came from or we could get the hell out! I mean, who taught us to be more responsible? To Nichole Grodski and Paul Wideman: thanks for opening your home to us and sharing time. Also to Nichole, individually for helping out with pictures for the book. Jeff Cochran for making it cool to build bad ass bikes on a budget again and for everything he does at Cycle Source. Thanks to Darren from Liquid Illusions for the piece on Roadside's paint on "Chick Magnet." Thanks to Easy and the rest of the Pensacola crew who took us in while we worked down there. Matt and Carl Olsen for the help in figuring out old bike stuff. A big, big thanks to John at Primo Rivera for taking our old SU and making it kick ass and road ready for the Pan. Dave Perewitz for the constant words of encouragement; you are a true OG my man! Donny Loos for over the phone Pan advice, and being a brother these many years. Carl at Cycle Electric for the greatest electrical system components on the planet. Tail End Customs for the coolest piston taillight on the "Ticket to Ride." Thanks to S&S Cycle for making quality American made products for home and shop builders to rely on. The entire Klock crew for constant support. Amy at Wizard Products who helped us learn to clean a bike the right way. J&P Cycles for tech help and overnight parts service. Thanks to Rollin Karol from Spectro Oils for their dedication to products for American motorcycles and our industry. Ed Fish Machine, DLK, Greco Welding Supply and Bakerstown Radiator for their help. Metzeler who provides the only tires we use in the Source Garage. Marilyn Stemp of Ironworks magazine who believed in me before I ever believed in myself. Thanks to Keith Ball who has been a true inspiration for all of us and of course, Timothy Remus for giving us the chance to put this book together. We hope it is all we promised it to be for you Tim.

Big love to our families, Robert Wideman, Nichole Grodski, Sam and Riley Wideman for their support. To Jean Munier, who keeps the magazine running while we go off on side projects like this book, and had to proof the whole damn thing since Chris can't spell. She also let me take over the second half of our shared space for the Source Garage.

To all the companies who advertise in *Cycle Source,* we send a big thanks for helping us deliver our message; it has been a great ride. Special thanks to everyone who has anything to do with organizing a swap meet. The meets are the true first steps for people to get into building bikes and to everyone from Long Beach to Davenport, we thank you for keeping this going.

Finally, thanks to all the *Cycle Source* readers who are in part made up of Garage Builders from every corner of the globe. Who would have thought that the little free newspaper deal we started fifteen years ago would have gone so far. It's only through your stories and from your support that we get to do it all so thank you all!

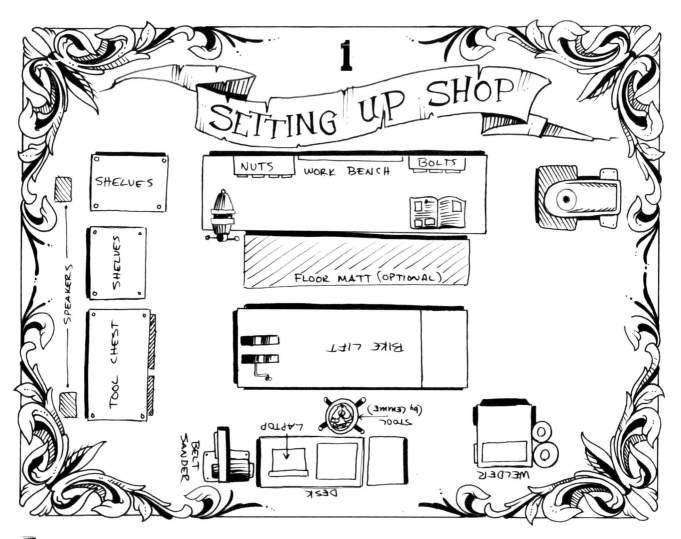

1
SETTING UP SHOP

SHELVES

NUTS   WORK BENCH   BOLTS

SPEAKERS

SHELVES

FLOOR MATT (OPTIONAL)

TOOL CHEST

BIKE LIFT

BELT SANDER

LAPTOP

STOOL (by ERMIE)

DESK

WELDER

They say that admitting you have a problem is step one, but in the world of customizing a bike, that is a given. Our first step recommendation, other than getting a Sugar Mama that might help pay for this menacing motorcycle addiction, is to set up the right environment to perform the work. Now whether you have a giant 60 x 60 space or your work area is confined to a small part of the basement, you can make the most of that area by having a solid plan, knowing what your budget is and of course it helps if you randomly collect things over the years for this purpose.

 To begin with, you are going to need to think about organization. The number one enemy of working efficiently, and this will be important if you are doing this part time, is to make tools, parts and supplies readily accessible. For this part of the book, we are going to work with my space. It's a 24 x 24 area in my garage and I started by covering all the walls with pegboard. It's cheap and easy to move things around on as your purpose sees fit. A flat black paint job helps chrome tools and parts stand out as well.

I had already made accommodations for electricity but this is a factor too. Nothing sucks as bad as not having outlets where you need them or having everything on the same circuit so that when you run a grinder, the lights go dim. Think it out; you're starting from square one so make sure it will be what you need in the long term.

Next step was the workbench. I had enough room for three, four foot work

Chris and the guys working in the Source Garage in Tarentum, Pennsylvania.

A quick fix for a simple insulated garage wall is to cover it with peg board.

benches, allowing more wall space for other tools. When you are putting in the bench or benches, the most important thing to remember is comfort. I asked a few people for advice on bench height to this end and found an actual formula does exist. Standing next to your bench with your hand bent at your wrist, you should be able to put your hand down flat on the top of the bench without bending your elbow, or just having a slight bend. Regardless of what anyone tells you, this will provide a good height for standing and working as well as sliding a stool up to the bench. Long hours of sanding or tedious work on small parts can really take a toll on your back and shoulders if you're not comfortable first. I also put a full shelf about half way to the floor for plenty of additional parts storage. It's amazing how much stuff you will start to squirrel away when you have a project or two going on. Having good space for that and for parts that come and go from platters and painters is key to keeping your stuff nice.

On top of your workbench you will want to mount a good solid vise. Remember to pick an area that will not cause you to curse the day you were born if you get a long piece of material in it and realize you're banging it off the walls. One trick here is to add an additional 2 x 4 to the

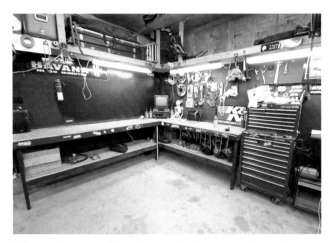

There is actually a formula for work bench height. Think storage and comfort for this step.

Our vise is not mounted correctly in this pic. It's recommended that you use an extra 2x4 to get it out away from the bench.

Two shop lights per circuit can give you lighting in the specific area you need it.

Most of my tools are Craftsman, but you should consider what is best for your budget and comfort.

Consider the placement of things like the compressor and the heater as well. Over in the corner or in another room to get them out of the way is choice.

front of the bench where you intend to mount the vise, and then run your front bolts down through it. This gives you additional clearance beyond the edge of the bench.

Working at the bench also requires sufficient lighting. Since you will most likely be working in your shop afterhours, don't rely on the amount of natural light that may come through any windows. In my shop we ran six, eight foot double row fluorescents across the entire shop ceiling and then each section of the workbench has its own four foot hanging shop light, a total of six with two separate circuits. This gives me the ability to have direct overhead light at any station I am working at on the benches.

Comfort will or should dictate many of your choices in setting up your work space. You should have some form of climate control no matter what part of the country you live in. When you have a comfortable work space you will work longer and it will be less tedious but keeping the garage at a constant temperature is good for other reasons as well. You see, when you go from the cold of the outside, to the warm inside, and then let it drop to the outside temperature again, it begins a cycle of condensation. This condensation will make bare steel parts' rust, bearings' seize and chrome parts will begin to pit. You have to consider spending some money up front to save on wasted parts and time in the long run.

A good selection of the basic tools, metric and American should be mentioned here. If you want to get it all at once, Sears offers nice packages. That and a decent toolbox will keep them organized and clean which is a must. Other tools that must be added as you get closer are: an electric grinder, full set of air tools, die grinder, DA sander, angle grinder, air driven wrenches, and paint sprayers. Trust me, after one ground-up custom, there isn't a tool in my garage that I haven't used. The further you get into this, a good bench-top grinder and a belt drive sander will come in handy more times than I can tell you. Remember, you don't have to do this all at once. Best practice is to get what you need as you need it.

One thing to consider right off the bat is the compressor. This is an area where I feel people tend to go too cheap. Most air tools that you will be using to grind and sand steel parts will require a minimum of 90psi to run effectively. This means that when you purchase the compressor, you want it to have a running psi of at least that much, more if you can afford it. The last thing you want when you are going to put 200 hours into smoothing out frame welds is a compressor that you have to stop and wait for. This work takes long enough so don't give yourself ammunition to burn the house down with in a late night fit of rage.

The installation of your air compressor is something else to consider. I have had compressors on the pallet they came on for years but the truth is they are quieter and safer to mount into the floor with lag bolts. It's an easy job with an impact drill, plus this will let you run steel lines around the shop so that you can have an airline coupler at each work station. A water filter and

regulator should be part of that airline system, right off the compressor, to ensure your tools will last a long time.

You will want at least one cabinet for frequently used chemicals. I used the traditional milk crate method for years but trust me, not having to pull out fifteen different crates to find the anti-seize you need for two bolts is worth the wall space of a cabinet. You may choose to take this a step further if you have the space and install a stand-up cabinet for sandpaper, large bottles of chemicals and fluids, small hand tools, etc. Speaking of chemicals, what about cleaning? Well, you can always just drag stuff out into the yard or driveway but this isn't practical and it's for sure going to kill the tree huggers in your neighborhood. You might just consider a cheap parts' cleaner as part of your start-up requirements. If you use the Simple Green solution, it also provides a place to wash hands at the end of the day, too.

So now we're getting close: you have some tools, a place to work, good lighting, storage, a clean-up station, some polishing tools, but what about a place for the motorcycle to be worked on? There is no two ways about it man, you got to have a stand. Now in my garage I finally have a killer Handy Lift and this pneumatic beauty

A little extra money for things like a dryer and regulator can make the best of your compressor.

Little wall cabinets are good to get started but you will want a nice big floor model before long.

You might want to keep more of your storage and less used items in the same location.

I am so serious about working on a lift that I have two of these Handy Lifts in my space now; one for short bikes and an extended one for choppers.

There are a lot of tools that you can make or rehab in the early stages of having a garage. I like my Daytona motor driven polisher more than a store bought version.

makes life so much easier. If that isn't in the budget, there are several other ways to go and they range from the $150 cycle jacks from Sears to just making a good stand out of wood on the cheap. The one thing we can't stress enough is that just sprawling this stuff out in the middle of the floor is a recipe for extreme aggravation, to your head and to your back.

And while we're on the subject of keeping to a tight budget, when I talk about the tools you must have, that doesn't mean you have to go out and buy these from Snap-On. There is no question of their quality but they can drag a brother into the poor house in a damn hurry if you're not careful. There are many other ways to acquire these items if you take your time. One is the swap meet and yard sale method which is self-explanatory. The weekly newspapers in your area are a good way to find both these types of sales as well as tools in general. Another great way to get by on a tight budget is to use what you have.

For my polisher I had this old Dayton furnace motor lying around for years. Instead of spending a couple hundred bucks on a polisher, I simply added a twenty dollar stand, two dollar switch and a couple of odds and ends to each end of the motor and poof, it polishes like a gem. You will find that the more of these actions you take, the more creative your builds will start to become as well. The foundation of custom bike building came from a time when there weren't catalogues full of parts for every make and model so cats back then used what they had and modified it to fit their purpose. It's good logic in this arena.

Nut and bolt storage should be on the list of things you want. If you are able to buy a set of hardware from a company like Gardner Wescott, I highly suggest it. This company has complete sets available in every finish and size you can imagine and even has a complete set of storage racks to keep it all organized.

Another way to do this is to have a set of plastic storage bins for this purpose. They are pretty cheap, stack nicely, they hold a ton of hardware and you can write on the outside of them. That and some of the new, fangled plastic coffee cans, yes I miss the old tin cans too, will do the job. In my case, I had been using option two for a long time until a brother of mine laid a set of the Gardner Wescott storage racks on me. It had a lot of hardware in it, some spaces were empty but it's a killer start on the next stage of my garage.

Keep a running wish list. This is a good idea so that friends and family always know what you have your eyes on for upgrades to the garage. A good drill press, an extra toolbox, and a tool cart for your immediate work area are all good additions to work towards. Believe it or not I will add in a TV and a DVD player here. While a good stereo is all you really need for garage entertainment, a TV and DVD combo will let you run "How To" videos close to the work where you can apply the lessons quickly while the information is fresh. They are not crucial to get started, but they can be time savers, and man, I can't imagine working without them now. Further down the road you might want to have some big items like your own lathe and maybe even a mill. Hope the ol' lady reads this book!

Over the course of the year that it took me to put this garage together to start building, I would end up spending approx $3,000. It may seem like a lot of cash but if you take into consideration the amount of money and time saved by not having to run all over town to borrow space to do the work, it's a sound investment. Furthermore, with the right workspace, and a good plan anyone with a nominal amount of mechanical ability, can learn to customize for themselves.

These bolt bins are nice because you can add to them over time, starting with the basics and adding a chrome or stainless assortment later.

Adding a drill press to my shop was a major score and made my work so much easier.

Today the Source Garage is my perfect space. From this pic I've added another table, a teardown table and a horizontal band saw... Oh, and a couch. I might end up moving out there.

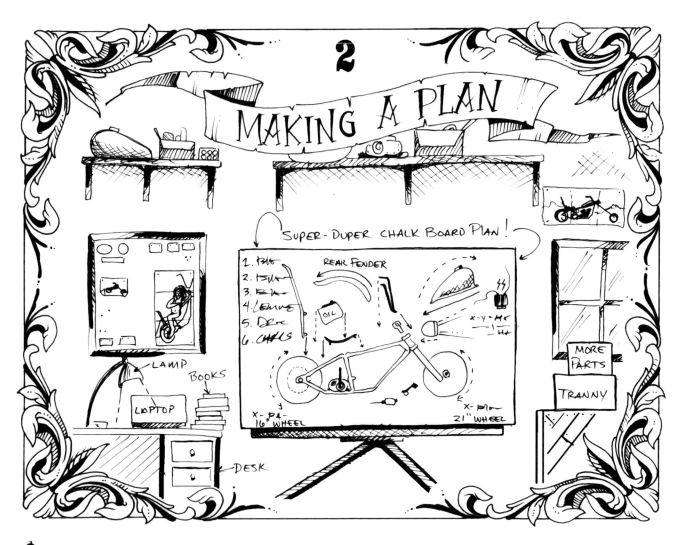

2

MAKING A PLAN

SUPER-DUPER CHALK BOARD PLAN!

One of the biggest mistakes made in the creation of a custom bike build is to just run out and start buying parts. I blame this on too much television making people believe that one thing or the other is cool so it should be the right choice for them. In this chapter, we will attempt to focus some of your creative urges and show you how to establish a plan of what you like and what you really want.

Take your time:

One of the easiest ways to make sure you are building the bike of your dreams, or at least the bike that you really want, is to take your time. There are thousands of parts available on the open market today for building custom bikes and probably at least a hundred categories of types and styles of bike builds. To really narrow down what it is you want to do, you might want

to start by picking an era.

Do you prefer a fifties-style traditional bobber with their big OEM style Springers? These bikes were customized by removing factory parts; they were lowered and made lighter to perform and handle better. Still, there is an iconic look about them that can be achieved without starting from a bone stock fifties' bike and to achieve this, you will need to research that era. Making friends within the Antique Motorcycle Club of America can go a long way into acquiring this knowledge as well.

Maybe a sixties/seventies era chopper is what you're after. If the long rail type chopper is the choice you make, then throw on some acid rock and kick back with some old Easyrider mags. This was the period that really started true radical customizing and from it, the aftermarket grew into a force that rivaled the OEMs. There are plenty of parts to go after this look but this style of bike is harder to build the right way than it may appear. It is not as simple as raking out the frontend and slapping a peanut tank on it. A true and proper seventies' chopper has to be ready to ride as well.

The eighties and nineties were a weird time for me, but maybe this time period yielded the type of custom bike you are after. There were several different styles that came out of the eighties and nineties. First were the swingarm customs that were being done to the last of the Shovelheads. They had custom parts that came partially from modifying parts from other bikes, and partially from the after-market. By the late eighties and early nineties, billet was starting to take over and colors were getting bright and crazy. Pro Street became all the rage, and names like Dave Perewitz, Donnie Smith and Ron Simms ruled the pages of all the top magazines.

As the new century came upon us, the "super choppers" hit the scene. The after-market was at its biggest point ever and

The best tool in any shop is the chair. This should be used from time to time to study where you are and where you're going.

Brother Speed is one of the cats who has taught me to slow down and take my time over the years.

Teach's bike Elvis is probably the perfect example of a traditional fifties bobber.

more choices were available to build with than any other time in the history of custom building. Bikes were being built to look like everything from jet planes and spider webs to helicopters and fire trucks. There is an entire library of media on these types of bikes and if this is what you are after, your research will be easy.

As the end of the first decade in the new century approached, the "old school" look was large and in charge. People were digging up ancient Shovels, Pans and Knucks like crazy. Bike events started to look a lot like they did in the seventies. Even the way cats were dressing resembled an entirely different period in time.

Again, a mass of media has been produced to highlight these types of bikes and it will not be hard for you to study their designs.

Books and Magazines:

Most of what I mentioned above was learned from the years that we have been producing Cycle Source as well as reading many of the other magazines over time. They are a great source for research into what style and specific parts you are looking for to build your custom since

S&S released the K-model a few years ago to meet their customer's demand for this style of bike.

most of their features come with a tech sheet to let you know what was used.

There have been scores of books produced over the past twenty years on custom bikes, many from the good people at Wolfgang, who have brought this work to you. A good book will site many of the build types and sources that we have talked about here.

The Internet and Television:

While these are both great sources to derive information from, they have to be used with a skeptic's eye. There is as much bad information on both as there is good so viewer beware. If you do like the Internet option, try and rely on a source with a community of people who participate on that site. This will give you a group sounding board for questions you might have. Television is basically junk food for the mind so for it, all I can say is you might see things you like.

Building Relationships:

As you begin to make your plan, I can't tell you how important it is to foster relationships with people who you can rely on for good information. You can start with local riders, local shop owners and the people who work for the catalogue companies where you will be buying parts. In the construction of my '49 Pan that you will see later in this book, the

Charlie Ransom's Evo powered chopper is a killer version of a long chopper and this one rides as good as it looks.

Adam's rail chopper shown here is a little longer and less well mannered in the ride department.

This sweet ass Evo built by Russell Marlowe capitalizes on the smooth lines and billet aluminum parts of the eighties and nineties.

relationship that I made with Jason, my parts' guy from Paughco, was essential to my plan. I had a pretty good idea of what I wanted but after many conversations with Jason, he went to the professionals at Paughco and came back to me with facts about the frame geometry that had to be considered. He knew what fit what and why not to use certain things I was asking for. I believe this bike to be what it is today largely because of Jason's help. There are other relationships we will talk about in later chapters that are essential like one with your local welding shop, steel yard and machine shop.

What Will You Start With:

There are three basic ways to build a custom bike. Knowing how you want to start will determine what the first part of your plan will be.

Swap Meet Rehab:

This is the process of finding a basket case (bike all in parts) or a bike that's nearly a basket as your foundation. This method requires a solid knowledge of motorcycle parts, their years and applications, as well as their value. It is extremely easy to get taken advantage of if you go into this

My boy Rick from Logic is a master of this style and his bikes are rolling works of art.

type of build without knowing what you are doing. Our brother and fellow staffer, Roadside Marty, is a master at the swap meet and you can see his rehab build later in this book as well.

Modified Aftermarket or Stock Build:

In this method, you simply add or remove parts from your stock bike to personalize it. This is a nice safe way to get into customizing and is made marginally more accessible by today's aftermarket. If you have never tried to build anything before, this is a good place for you to start. You won't have to worry about your bike's handling, performance or safety.

Ground-Up Custom:

This type of build starts with an idea and little more. Some of the parts for a ground-up can come from the aftermarket, like my '49, some can be acquired from the swap meet and some can be made from scratch like Paul Wideman's build that is in the last part of this book. A ground-up build should absolutely not be your first attempt at building a custom bike. This is a more advanced method of building and if you try this too soon, before you develop a skill set and become more comfortable with the work, it can cost you time and money, leaving you frustrated.

Mike Prugh's designs are unmistakable and his ability to carry out that new age style in the early change of the century was almost unmatched.

Some of the Custom Aftermarket Manufacturers like Big Dog and American Iron Horse were examples of this style. Although they were no where near as intense as a true one off custom, they were readily available and consumers grabbed them up.

A Physical Example:

Whether you can draw or work a computer to cut and paste a mock-up picture together, it's a good idea to have a physical example in front of you to outline what it is you are shooting for. Even if it is as simple as tearing pages out of magazines to hang on the garage wall, the inspiration that comes from studying the design concept of where you are going will be a constant guide to keep you on track. It also helps when you want to make modifications to your original plan. You can go to the reference model first to see if the modifications are sound before you spend any money or time.

Keeping a Good List:

A list of what tasks you have before you is not only a good idea to keep your project organized but is essential in not letting your build hit a flat spot. Each time you get to cross something off that list, you get a feeling of accomplishment. Times when waiting for things like chrome and paint may slow down your progress, you can see how far along you have come. A helpful tool to this end can be a dry erase board kept on the wall in your garage.

For me, no one gets this design concept as well as Jeff Cochran. He is the master.

A lot of the young guys like Bill Bryant whose bike is in the front here, really started to reach back and bring the old style back to life.

18

Setting a Deadline:

Rome for sure wasn't built in a day, but it wasn't built by cats who kept saying someday either. Having a deadline, even if it's a self-imposed deadline like wanting to make Willie's Tropical show in the spring, forces you to give the proper attention to your project. Plus, the more organized you are, the more likely you will be to not miss or skip anything. Time management is a huge part of getting things done in the right order and correctly so keeping a list and staying on schedule work hand-in-hand.

Establishing a Budget:

You may be well to be honest from the start about what you want to spend on your build. It is easy enough to calculate the cost of parts and supplies, in a ball park manner at least, to get a rough estimate of what the cost will be. By doing this, you can see how to save money on one thing that can be applied to another area. It will also keep you out of the dog-house with your significant other. In any event, the budget can be kept in the same notebook with your list. You will see very quickly that taking your time and planning things out in advance will cost way less than having to get parts or services from a machine shop in a hurry. This practice will also force you to be creative in some areas where it may be easier to buy a new part, but if the budget doesn't have room for that, you adapt and overcome. Instead, you can find an old part, modify it and come out ahead.

While there is a lot of fun in building a custom motorcycle, to do it successfully there is just as much management involved. Keeping track of your four resources; human, physical, financial, and informational, will keep you on track from start to finish, ensuring that you have the luxury of enjoying what you are building.

A regular diet of magazines is like a bad drug for the home bike builder. It will lead to creative thought and spending way too much time in the garage.

Mastering the swap meet is every young Jedi Ghetto Builder's true goal. It will take a lifetime so get started early.

I got a thousand ideas just from the last time I was at a Tropical Tattoo show during Bike Week. This source can not be overlooked.

19

3

LOVE THY WELDER

GAS

POWER SOURCE

TORCH TIPS

PORCELAIN TIPS

FOOTSWITCH

TORCH

So you're at the point where you are ready to put your plan into action. You've set up your shop just the way you want it, sourced the coolest, most desired parts in the land, and got your beautiful drivetrain waiting to be planted in its new home. You're ready. Or are you?

When your plan doesn't line up exactly with your parts' selection, you have but a few choices. You can source new parts, or make the ones you have work. For most of us, we choose to make our parts work. Oftentimes this requires cutting a good (or not so good) piece apart. Yes, this is a drag but that's what makes it custom. You cannot merely assemble a chopper and claim you built it. Welding is indeed a very daunting task to the new builder but I can assure you, once you have taken the time to learn this skill, and you fully embrace this hybrid of science and art, you will feel a

sense of accomplishment and separation from the "assemblers." And you will truly "Love Thy Welder."

Most of you have heard of the different forms of welding. From MIG to TIG, Gas Brazing to AC/DC Stick; we've all had an uncle or grandfather who had a set of torches or an old buzz box in the garage. But which form of welding best suits your shop, your budget, and your build?

Concerns and Considerations

There are a few major considerations you must take into account when deciding which welder will best fit your needs. First and foremost is safety. Will welding in your work space potentially harm you or your family? This is an obvious concern, and it must be properly addressed. Be sure there are sufficient fire extinguishers in the area. The kind of heat any welder generates is enough to make a flame out of nearly any building material if the proper steps are not taken. Ventilation is a major safety concern. Be sure that you have an exhaust fan if you plan to weld in an enclosed area. If you are in the garage, simply leaving a door open is not enough. Use a fan to draw the fumes out of the garage. Also, you must investigate whether your town, subdivision, etc. will allow your form of welding in a residential area. You don't want to wire in your new machine and gear up your new shop, only to have the powers that be stop by and tell you that you're on the wrong side of the law.

You also need to take a look at your service panel. Be sure that you know what power you have available prior to purchasing your welder. The most common entry level welders run on 220V, but many are available with a 110V power input. Do you already have 220V in your garage? If you do, you are already a few steps (and a few dollars) ahead. If not, you must decide to wire a 220V outlet to your workspace, or settle on a 110V unit. If you decide to go the 110V route, you will also need to check into the amperage rating of your outlets. Many household outlets are only rated to 15 amps, and your new welder may draw 30 or more amps. If you are lucky enough to have 220V in your workspace, it's probably a good idea to double check your amperage rating on the outlet. More than likely it will be sufficient, but check it anyway.

Size is also a concern. We have a welder in our shop that takes up nearly an entire bike size spot on the shop floor. You do not want that in your workspace if you can help it. Try to plan ahead when setting up your benches and account for a good place to park your weld rig when not in use. It would be nice if the welder is in an easily accessible area where you can

Here's a shot from the Source Garage. You can see the welder is close to the electric panel and has an extension to reach anywhere in the shop.

Paul Wideman shown here TIG welding a custom set of exhaust pipes.

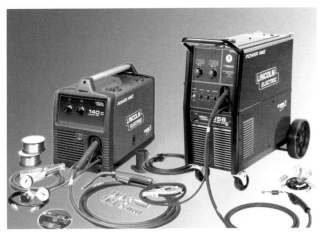

At left, Lincoln makes a nice line of smaller MIG machines that are inexpensive and serve as good little work horses. The larger machines (at right) are better for a wider range of work. Ask your local dealer for advice on what will suit you best.

Ahh the heat wrench. No matter what of the many uses you may find for this tool, there is little chance your shop will be complete without one.

pull your leads to any corner of the shop without having to uproot other tables, benches, or tools. Also, when you purchase your welder, consider a good cart for both the unit and the gas cylinder. You can also choose to build one to suit your taste; after all, you have a welder.

MIG or GMAW

MIG is the most common type of welder used in the home garage. Gas Metal Arc Welding, or GMAW, has been around for over 70 years. The process uses an electric arc to heat the metals. This arc is between the base material(s) and a continuous, consumable electrode (wire). Atmospheric contaminants are shielded from the weld by a shielding gas. While it was originally used to join non-ferrous materials such as aluminum, it has since been adapted to steels and other materials. MIG is widely preferred for its versatility and ease of use. You'll find one in every body shop in the country. Please do not confuse a MIG machine with a wire feed welder. While they are very similar, the wire feed welder must use a flux core wire and will not allow use of a shielding case. A MIG machine can use flux core wire if need be, thus eliminating the need for a shielding gas. The MIG process will result in a far superior weld than the flux core process.

There are many quality MIG machines out there that will allow you the portability you need to get around all sides of your bike during the fabrication process, and still have enough power to provide a consistent, proper weld, all while not taking up an entire corner of your garage. There are also larger machines that will allow even more versatility and higher output ratings, but they are generally more expensive and will take up more space on your garage floor. This is where you need to define your needs and resources and decide which machine is best for your situation.

One of the few drawbacks to the MIG machine is the mess it creates. Your motorcycle is your art piece. You do not want spatter and huge weld beads all over your work. The spatter can be reduced by one of many anti-spatter products out there. Additionally, MIG welding can tend to be fairly porous, and is therefore not ideal for work that requires leak testing. You can drive yourself crazy chasing down leaks in a MIG weld. You are also limited to the size and detail of the area you are welding. Sometimes the bead that the MIG process creates will detract from the piece you have fabricated. This may lead you to a different process.

Gas Welding and Brazing

Gas welding, or oxy/fuel welding has been around since the early 1900s. Gas welding uses pure oxygen and fuel to weld and cut. Oxygen is used rather than air, as oxygen will create a considerably higher temperature. The beauty of an oxy/fuel rig is the versatility. You can weld, cut, anneal, braze, heat and form with a single tool. For this reason, it is recommended that any serious bike builder invest in a quality oxy/fuel setup at the earliest convenience.

A torch rig takes up very little space in your garage, and requires no electrical service. You can also purchase or build a cart to roll your torches around on, making them very portable. A long lead is also a plus, so you can reach any area of your shop in short order. Gas welding is a great way to join materials of both similar or dissimilar metals, as well as thin weldments, such as sheet metal. The downside to the oxy/fuel path is the time and practice it takes to become proficient with every aspect of this form of welding/cutting. Do not let that deter you, however; you MUST learn to use this very important tool.

TIG or GTAW

Gas Tungsten Arc Welding, or TIG, is the welding process in which a dedicated, nonconsumable tungsten electrode produces an arc, while being shielded by an inert gas. A filler metal is usually added independent of the welder itself. TIG welding is the most precise and strongest form of welding in the motorcycle world. Dating back to the early 1940s, TIG welding allows the fabricator to use focused heat and reduce cleanup time. If coupled with a remote power control, the oper-

The Source Garage is equipped with this exact TIG unit from Lincoln. It's a fantastic unit and serves us well for the aluminum job we do once in a while also.

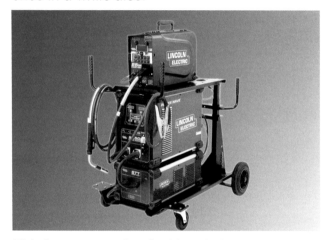

This is an example of a Lincoln inverter type machine. This is probably way over the top for the home shop.

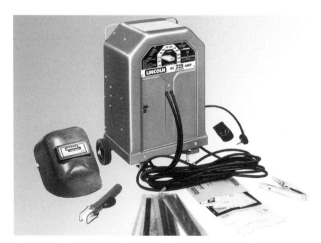

Arc welding machines like this one from Lincoln are widely used in small shops today and have been for quite a while.

ator can continuously increase or decrease the output amperage as needed. One drawback to TIG welding is the degree of difficulty; it takes a lot of practice to become a proficient TIG welder.

There are basically two types of TIG power sources to consider for your home shop: the rectifier type machine and the inverter type. The rectifier power source uses bulky transformers to turn the input power into the desired output. For the home builder, a rectifier machine is suitable and a reasonably priced choice. A quality rectifier machine will cost you a little more than a MIG machine of equal quality.

The inverter power source is a much more versatile and powerful unit than the rectifier machines. An inverter power supply greatly boosts the input frequency, reducing the number of coils needed to transform input power into output power. This results in a much lighter and smaller machine. An inverter machine allows the user greater adjustability and many options for wave shape. If there is any downside to the inverter TIG machine, it is simply the price. A quality inverter rig will cost

you many times that of a rectifier unit or MIG machine.

AC/DC Arc Welding

Arc or stick welding is the oldest of the contemporary welding techniques. There is a reason for this, as stick welding is very strong, versatile, inexpensive, and relatively easy to learn. Arc welding uses a power supply to create an arc between the electrode and the base metal. Either flux or a shielding gas must be used to prevent contaminants from entering the weld area. TIG welding is a form of arc welding.

In the motorcycle world, however, stick welding is a bit out of place. It is certainly strong enough, but it creates a large bead and a lot of slag. You will also have a lot more mess and fumes in your shop. Luckily most TIG machines have a "stick" option, allowing you to run a stick welding electrode instead of the TIG torch. This is very handy when building tables, benches, or even a cart to roll your welder around on.

Gear

A decent hood is a must. There are many fancy options out there, but the most important part in choosing a hood is comfort. You need to find something that will fit your head comfortably and securely. Find a good supply house and ask to try their hoods on. Don't jump right to the auto-shade hoods. While they do serve a great purpose, they also have their drawbacks. When welding in tight areas, the sensors can be shielded and you will be flashed. Get used to welding with a traditional hood before moving up to an auto-shade; I waited 17 years to get one. If you are only gas welding, a good set of goggles with

Here is a nice selection of the custom welding hoods available from Lincoln Electric.

interchangeable lenses is a good idea.

The type of gloves you choose depends on the type of welding you are doing. Arc and MIG welding require you wear a thicker glove to prevent spatter from getting through to your hands. While TIG and gas welding you will want a thinner material, such as deer skin, so you can better feel your filler rod.

This same approach applies to your clothing. Be sure that you are not wearing anything that it is flammable, especially when MIG or arc welding. There are numerous suppliers of weld jackets and aprons. Find a good one, one that fits tight and is comfortable.

You should always wear safety goggles. While you are welding, you are of course protected by the hood, but after you remove the hood, there is the possibility of gas trying to escape and a weld "popping." This can send hot metal straight into your unprotected eyes. So, always protect your eyes.

Now What Do I Do?

After you've gotten your new welding rig and all of your gear, you need to start learning how to use all of it. You CANNOT just jump in and start welding parts on your bike. You must have strong, safe welds. This does not just mean running your welder as hot as it can go without burning through the base metal. There is a science to it, and I strongly recommend taking a course at your local community college or Vo-tech school. There is a ton of information in books and on the Internet that will help you as well.

There are only three things you need to remember if you want to improve at welding: practice, practice, practice.

In Closing

Become friendly with your local welding supply house. They are a vital source of information. Any time you have a question about filler material, shielding gas, new or unfamiliar processes, they are there to help. You are also likely to find other resources there as well, such as a good machine shop that can help you out.

And practice!

As far as gloves go it depends on what you are comfortable with. Heavy ones like these will protect you better.

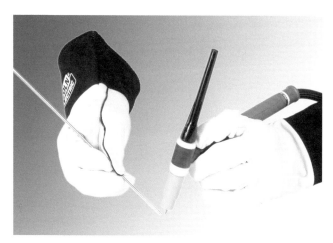

On the other hand, Lincoln makes thin gloves now that are better for more intricate work and still offer a good level of protection.

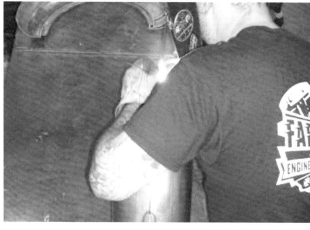

Paul is shown here TIG welding two halves of a fender blank together.

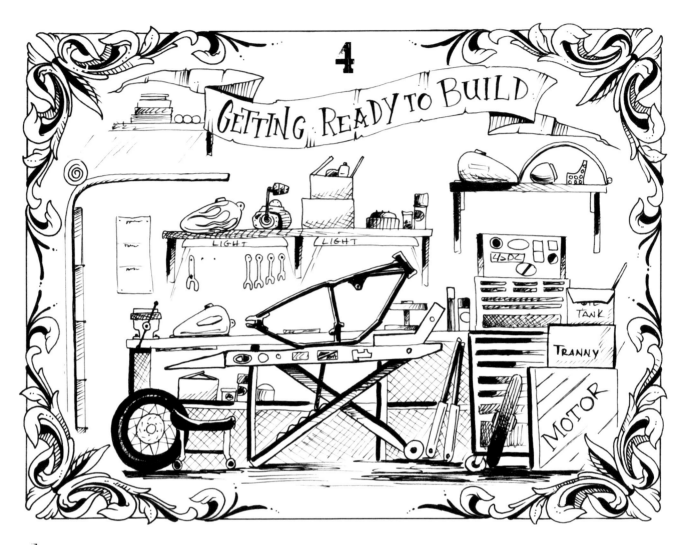

4
GETTING READY TO BUILD

OK, so you have the tools and the space to build your custom bike, you have a solid plan and you know what you want to build, but are you ready to build? Getting ready to build is a lot more involved than just waiting for those first few boxes of parts to arrive at your shop. There is, in fact, a long list of things to get ready to make sure you will have the time, money and support required to move forward without any major setbacks.

Making Relationships:

So this is something that you should pick up over the years, but there are a few key relationships that you will want to make sure you have in place before you start to build. We already brought this up in a previous chapter, but the following will provide more of a breakdown on the importance of who you know. Not knowing everything is not a problem as long as you have access to information from peo-

ple who do. For the most part, the motorcycle community is pretty good about passing on information if you are ready to learn. So in the scheme of your build, let's take a look at a few of the resources you may want to develop.

A Welding Supply Shop:

As we will talk about in depth, in the next chapter, the guys at your local welding supply shop can be one of your best assets. When I started to learn the art of TIG welding, they helped me with everything from the basics to where to turn for more information. It all started when I finally got my Lincoln Power TIG fired up. Since I didn't set it up myself, a friend had installed a bottle of gas for me. It was in fact the wrong type of gas, a mixture of two gases instead of straight Argon, the preferred gas for TIG welding. After putting that advice to good use, my welding started to progress much faster. They also helped me with proper tip selection for work I was doing And in talking with them later, when I mentioned the problem I was having with the low grade steel I was using, and they suggested a local steelyard.

Steel Yard:

A good steelyard is an absolute must for building custom bikes and parts. Finding one like I have in my neighborhood is a dream. They are a company by the name of Metco Steel in Leechburg, PA and the nicest thing

It's hard to believe that we already have about 100 hours in the frame at this point but it's true. The time goes fast so get ready!

about them is they are a specialty yard of sorts. See, if I need a certain length of ¼ inch steel plate, not only will they search their leftover stock but they will cut it to length for me as well. This saves huge amounts of time for anyone who doesn't have a lot of tools and might have to cut with an electric grinder and a cut off wheel. They also have a real nice catalogue of products that are laid out with prices per foot, helping you keep to a budget. They will make suggestions on what products and thicknesses they think are required for what type of application; if you are adding a structural piece into a frame you don't want the gauge of steel to be too light.

A Machine Shop:

Unless you are starting off with way more resources than a traditional beginner might have, namely a lathe and a milling machine, then having a good machine

A true machinist like Craig here is a lifesaver. Not only can they get you the best result, they can get you out of a bad spot in a hurry.

The welding supply store we go to takes the time with us to teach us about products or applications we don't know.

A specialty steel yard like the one we deal with can save you tons of time and money by cutting your material to length.

Having a machine shop close to your shop will save time, but make sure first and foremost you're confident in their work.

shop at your disposal is critical. In my case, Ed Fish Machine is the go-to operation for all things requiring skill in the machine arts. They do a solid job, like many shops you can find, but the real deal is the relationship. You see the owner, Ed, is a hot rod and bike builder on the side. He's had one of each in issues of Cycle Source and builds an incredible machine whether it has two or four wheels. Knowing this is his background gives me a leg up when it comes to part fabrication. Since he has a firm grasp of the components on a motorcycle, it's that much easier to convey my ideas to him with rough drawings, templates and measurements. It also gives my a little edge when it comes to turnaround too. Since Ed builds, he knows how bad it sucks to wait for parts and I think he always hurries my stuff through because of that.

A Good Supply Source:

No matter where you buy your supplies, online or at a brick and mortar joint, a person-to-person relationship is a good start. Now, once you begin to acquire the basic knowledge of what tools and supplies you will be using are available, it will be easier for you to buy from MSC or Eastwood, but for the time being, going to a local auto body supply shop might be the best place to start. In my situation DLK Performance in Russelton, PA is that shop and in addition to good prices and good information, they have also turned me on to places to buy products they don't sell. And new ways to achieve the solutions and results I was looking for. Even on a basic level, asking these guys questions like, what's the best way to finish mild steel to prep it for any finish, will give you good ideas from people who know.

This is where you will start to learn about the use of flapper wheels and tapers. A flapper wheel is a disc for the electric grinder that comes in several different grits like sandpaper. Tapers are cone shaped sanding tips that can be used on the end of a die grinder that also come in different grits; these things are great for tight spots. And last but not least, the power of the DA sander, that when used in conjunction with the previously mentioned tools, can finish your metal for chrome, powdercoating or paint just like the pros.

Professional Shop:

Now you might have to search for a while until you find the right type of custom bike shop that can answer your questions; some of these dudes can be downright pricks who protect their information. Hey, it's how they make a living so keep in mind, the best way to form a relationship with them is to make them part of your process, in short, spend some money there. Even if you can get all your parts on e-Bay or by other imported shitty ways, try and remember the mom and pop bike shops and custom builders who hang a shingle are the libraries of information you need and that our culture exists on.

Brothers, Friends and Neighbors:

They say that it takes a village to raise a child; well it takes a whole group of people to actually build a bike. There are no two ways about this one. You may be able to build a custom bike by yourself but it will take you much longer and will frustrate you at times to a level that I swear by all things holy is unknown to you at this point. Face it, it's not only nice to have someone hold something for you when you're working at a difficult angle but it's a blast to share the experience with them as well. There is a combined knowledge base achieved by working with other people, whether you think they have more experience than you or not. Having someone else involved gives you the benefit of a fresh perspective and can make tasks easier just by changing the way you think about them. In my case, I add in as many people as I can. Having extra hands saves time and if you are building after hours, in between work and family, it can get a little freaky. Getting more done in less time can be a major difference in coming out with your backside intact.

Made In America:

Originally, I wasn't sure if I wanted to put this part in but I feel compelled to. In this day and age, we have to humbly suggest buying

It always comes down to the person behind the counter. Our guy at DLK is never too busy to hear a stupid question, and it's a good thing.

Flapper wheels on an electric grinder can get you amazing results. Wearing the glove while using one instead of going to the hospital from being dumb can save time!

See, Lemme is a pro and has gloves, glasses and man can he get the work out the door!

Building a bike is a family affair where I come from. Everyone shows up at one point or another to lend a hand.

Paul Wideman shows an example of the age old art of fender spinning here. Some things you just can't get in this kind of quality over seas.

Buyer beware, the swap meet can save or cost you a bundle depending on how much you know going in.

American made parts for your build at any opportunity you can. I know that tough times call for tough decisions but on behalf of all we are in the custom motorcycle scene in the United States, this is just a simple reminder that American jobs depend on your purchases; enough said.

The Swap Meet:

This section has been put at the end for the chapter not because it's the last in the list of importance, but because it requires most of the resources above. You see, just going to the swap meet doesn't give you anything other than a selection of used parts. Knowing what you are looking at can only be achieved through years of being around this stuff or by a solid relationship with people who have.

There are books out there on part fitment that can help you acquire this knowledge as well. One I would suggest for anyone building Shovelhead based customs or older, is from Mike Arman. He book is titled What Fits What, which is a parts' interchange and performance handbook for Harley-Davidson motorcycles from 1936 through 1983. This is great resource and can be the foundation of what you are building.

Knowing what it costs to repair something from a swap meet, whether it is a broken fin on a head or cylinder that might need to go to the machine shop, or a rebuild on a transmission that a local bike shop can do, is also important.

Common sense is an essential asset when it comes to navigating the swap meet. Taking a friend with you who has more experience is an excellent way to avoid buying parts that turn out to be unwanted junk. Try not to be too damned eager just because you see a pair of shovel heads. Don't run up with that look a teenager gets flipping through his old man's '70s biker rag collection. Take your time and look them over, ask questions and walk around. If you're looking at something, don't just take for granted that things will work out because it's the right part for your year and make. Really take a good hard look at it and check for signs of wear, missing mounting hardware or damaged threads on mounting studs. Each item that goes on a list of "work to be done to a part from the swap meet" takes away from its value and adds to your budget in time and money. For God's sake don't just take someone's word that an engine or transmission has just been rebuilt. Simple signs can tell you the real story like if the gaskets look new or old, or if the Allen head bolts are clean looking or are filled with debris.

The modern day swap meets are far from the former greatness they used to be; many of them today will be comprised of much more take-off parts. While this makes it harder to find the great part you're looking for to fit your old bike, it also has some benefits. One way to look at the positive here is that a lot of this stuff can be modified to fit your build and save you a ton of money for what are effectively new parts most of the time.

Getting Royally Screwed Is Still The Best Lesson:

Now this might be hard to believe but no one who does this is immune from getting screwed at least once in a royal method. Roadside himself, a brother that I consider a master of the swap meet and low budget rocker, even had his day at bat. He shared a story with me about the first set of $800 pan heads that he had to have because he wanted to build his first Pan. He snatched these things up and ran off with them like had found gold, only to be disappointed to see, upon closer examination that they were absolute junk and only good enough for cutting fins off of to weld on to otherwise good heads. Every D-ring hole was stripped and there was epoxy holding the exhaust ports together: an absolute mess. Now you could go on the warpath and do some time over beating this dude up but the best medicine is to take it like a man and learn from you mistakes. A little bit of pain right now and the next time you will never have to worry about making the same mistake. As for me and the '49, I didn't get screwed but I did end up with some mis-

matched stuff and had to spend more time sorting it out. Had I known what I was looking at in the beginning... well, who are we kidding, I still would have snatched them up. I mean, it was a perfect set of '49 cases with paper!

I still remember this day like I had just picked up my first bike ever. It was my first Pan, and so the lessons began.

Loose studs and peeled chrome was only part of the problem with my old four speed. It could have been worse though.

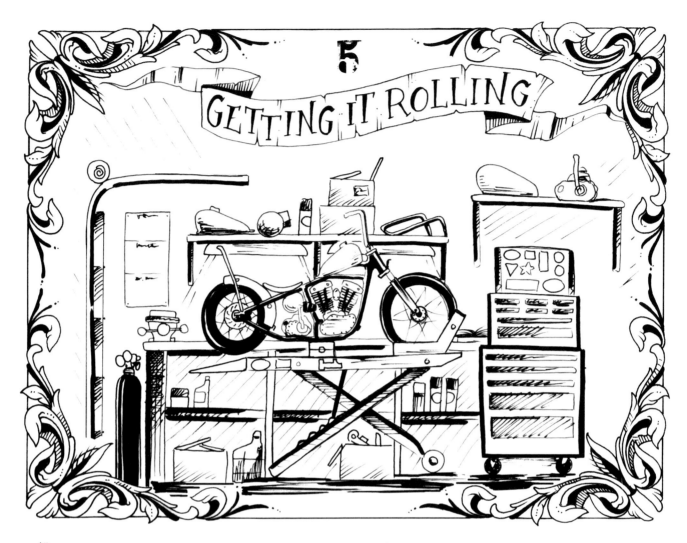

GETTING IT ROLLING

5

Getting your build to the point where it's a rolling chassis is one of the most satisfying parts of the project. Many people will argue about exactly when this should happen, but for our purpose we like to do this almost before anything else. By getting the frame, frontend, wheels and handlebars assembled, even in a rough state, you will be able to get a real look at what the stance of the bike is going to be. This is crucial because if the bike doesn't stand as tall in the frontend as you had planned or envisioned, you can make alterations to your plan as far as the fuel tank goes to make up for that. Maybe you intended to use a deep tunnel fuel tank and now seeing your roller, you think a shallow tunnel, to put the tank up higher, will give you more of the stance you are looking for. Much of the motorcycle's personality is based on this stage of

the build so take your time and really look at what you have in your rolling chassis and how it does or does not fit your plan. In this chapter, we will go over some of the fundamentals that are required to get your bike to the point where it's a roller. It's not as easy as just buying some stuff and throwing it together, but it shouldn't be looked at with the fear of an ancient culture looking at a solar eclipse. Let's start with the wheels.

Wheels and Tires:

By this point, you should have already looked over what your choices in wheels are, considered what would be the best fit for the frame you are using will be and what tires will look the best for what you are building. In today's world, the tire design does as much for pulling out a bike's personality as anything else.

A square, old style chopper tire, like a Shinko will give you just that: an old chopper look. On the other hand, an aggressive tread pattern like the dual sport that ACME used on one of their Choppers will give you a much more rough-and-ready looking bike.

At this point, it is important to consider the fenders too because not all tire and fender combinations will work well together.

For our '49 Pan, we chose a Metzeler ME880 for the rear since it would fill up the fender nicely, didn't have an aggressive tread and is very reliable. In the end, this bike is gonna be a rider so that factor was important to us.

Assuming you now have the right tire and wheel combination worked out ahead of time, and the fender design fits well with these components, what options do you have for customizing here? Well, there are many things you can do with used or even new spoke wheels. You can take them apart and have the hubs painted, chromed or powder-coated.

You can do the same with the rims, or as in our case, you can swap out the stock hub for a spool wheel. You can see the steps of this in a later chapter but the end result was a wheel that is a step above what can be bought off the shelf, and that's custom.

Similar things can be said here for billet wheels or just figuring out how to use wheels from other bikes and

Store bought rollers like this one from Sucker Punch Sallys are a breeze for the builder because they have already been fit with the proper wheel spacers.

Keeping a list of what tire design and size combinations you run across on other builds you like can help you with future projects.

Getting that correct fit can be impossible with a tire that doesn't go with the style of fender you are using.

Proper radius can be adjusted to get a better fit but it does take more time.

The entire personality of a bike can come down to the tread patten, believe it or not.

These little spool hubs from JR's Cycle are a great way to customize a stock wheel.

If you have started with the tire you may have to consider switching to a different style of fender all together.

Here are the custom made rear wheel spacers for our '49 Project.

adapting them to fit your particular application. This is another great place for advice from one of your relationships with a local expert.

So let's assume that you have the wheels figured out and you're ready to move on to getting them spaced out in the frame. In spite of what you see in the parts' books, you may not find exactly what you need in a spacer kit, but it's a good place to start. Otherwise it's off to the machine shop with your measurements for a custom made set of spacers.

Paughco sells a nice 28-piece kit that includes two each of 14 different length polished chrome steel spacers from 1/4 to 3 inches in length and the kit comes in 3/4 and 1 inch I.D. But let's talk for a minute about why these spacers are important. First and foremost, the spacer performs a crucial mechanical role. Its function is to shoulder the bearings of the wheel on one side and the

frame on the other, allowing the axle to be tightened down. This permits the bearing to spin freely without any obstruction. The correct spacing also ensures proper wheel alignment for handling and the fitment of parts around the wheel, like the chain, fenders, etc.

Let's start with the basics on spacers with the rear wheel. For this step you want to have your axle, brake mount, rotor and wheel in place.

To begin with, you will want to run a string or laser line, if you have the means for that, from the center of the rear wheel to the center of the neck on the frame. Following the line all the way up the backbone and making sure the wheel is centered on the axle will give you the spacers you need on both sides of the wheel.

By using a caliper, you can slide the caliper out and take a measurement of what each spacer should be. If you're not sure how to read a caliper, then transferring these

Kiwi Mike matched his sprocket Hub and Rim color here for a great result on an Indian board track racer.

Even painting a stock wheel like Twisted Choppers did on this Buell can give it a custom look.

The string method of centering the wheel on the backbone is shown here.

To get a measurement for your own custom made spacers start with your axle, brake mount, rotor and wheel on the bike.

Once the wheel is centered, you just measure the space you need to fill.

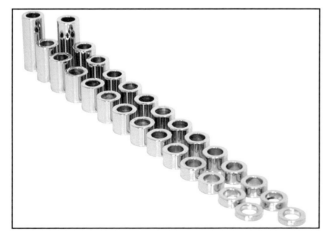

Paughco's wheel spacer kit is a great way to start for anyone who doesn't have ready access to a machine shop.

I haven't been reading a caliper for that long so transferring to a tape helps me at the machine shop.

results to a tape measure is easy enough.

One important thing to remember here is that you are going for the exact fit. The last thing you want to do is have either too much space or too little, putting undo flex on the rear section of the frame. Either condition will result in extra stress that can lead to cracking in the frame and a major repair down the road. To avoid this, make sure that the spacers slide in without a lot of force and that they also do not fall in with no resistance.

Repeat this step for the front wheel and once all the measurements are in hand, you can either go to the local machine shop and have spacers made from scratch, take the spacers from your builder kit that are closest and have them machined to spec, or if you are as lucky as we were with our front wheel on the '49, find the spacers that fit your measurement.

With the correct spacers in hand, you can now mount the tires on the wheels and install them on the bike. Once you get the bike on the floor, the real work begins. This is a good time to have a nice fat chair in your shop because setting the bike on its kickstand and just going from side to side, to sit and stare, is good medicine. Really take the time at this point to look it over and be honest with yourself about what you think. Trust me, skipping through this process in the rush to move on can result in a plain old, ugly-ass bike. One that will never make you happy. The problem is; by the time this really starts to hit, you may be so far into the build that redoing part of the bike just isn't practical. A little time spent now adjusting the plan can pay off big in the end result.

This is a good time to pull out the fuel tank and look at how it sits on the backbone. Does it compliment the lines of the frame or does it stick up like it's out of place? You may also do well to start thinking about clearance issues here too. Does the frontend swing from one side to another without banging into the tank? Can you see where the pipes will be, the foot controls, etc? Do you have enough ground clearance from the frame geometry to make this bike ride-able? If you answer no to any of these or even if you are not sure, STOP moving ahead and ask for another opinion. I know it's a painful proposition to move backwards this early, but it may be the difference between having a safe, good looking motorcycle or riding around on an uncomfortable rolling turd that gets you no admiration from any of your peers.

Here are some of Paughco's premade pacers installed. Nice fit and a nice finish.

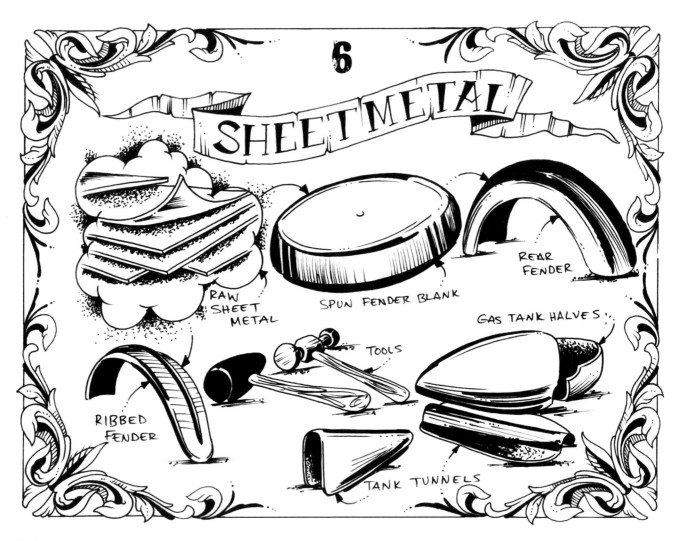

6

SHEET METAL

RAW SHEET METAL

SPUN FENDER BLANK

REAR FENDER

GAS TANK HALVES

TOOLS

RIBBED FENDER

TANK TUNNELS

"To fab or not to fab," should really be the question. Now, if you have some experience in the metal arts and understand what the tools are and how to use them, hand fabbing sheet metal can give your bike an unmistakable look that will not be lost in the crowd. Since this is a book on customizing basics, we are going to move forward under the assumption that you do not have the experience to tackle a task like this and will start with things you can get or may have around the shop already.

Store Bought Parts:

Okay, so just like some of the other things we've talked about in this offering, buying parts from an aftermarket or OEM supplier isn't a bad option because of the advantages they build into them, but they sure aren't parts of a real custom build until you put some love into them either.

Rehab Parts:

Some of the coolest sheet metal creations I've ever seen have been made from old banged up stuff that other people were throwing away. Stretching out sporty tanks, cutting them apart and adding in new tunnels for depth and using fenders from other makes and models is a great start to customizing. Again, we can point out some of the benefits: factory parts usually fit better and are better engineered than some aftermarket parts, and they are for sure better than you may be able to make out of the gate, by hand.

I remember one time we were building a Softail chopper, 45 degrees of rake, with a big deer-killer front wheel on it, and I wanted the backend to be smaller so it came back to more of a point. When we looked around for a rear fender, we ended up taking a wrecked

FLH front fender, turning it around and adding two inches to the center of it. A little bit of on and off and adjusting and we had a very unique, cool ass fender. We welded in a nice oval taillight housing and sent it off to paint.

In our case with the '49, seen at the back of the book, my sheet metal consisted of a peanut tank like the one from the Captain America chopper and a flat strap rear fender, both acquired from Paughco. Now the tank was pretty much what I wanted as far as the look. Other than the surface finish and sealing, all we changed was the way it mounted to the frame. This required no changes to the tank but more on the end of the frame, mounting hardware and positions, which we'll get into later in this book.

The fender was another case entirely. To use the common flat strap or trailer fender that is so widely used in custom builds today, there is a considerable amount of work to make them really look good on a bike. You could always just slap some mounting holes on it and go with it, but one of the main things you need to do to have a truly customized flat strap is to radius it to the size of your rear wheel.

This will give us the opportunity to go over some of the tools used in real world sheet metal fabrication, albeit on a more advanced level than in regu-

Bare Knuckle Choppers supplies a ton of the aftermarket suppliers with fenders and were a huge help in my sheet metal schooling.

It's hard to believe that 90 days from this picture there would be a finished motorcycle. Try not to set that pace for your project.

Cycle Warehouse became my regular haunt during the three months I was working on the '49. Old parts, new parts, you'll need to get to them fast.

One of my previous builds, just an old Softail with a 45 degree rake and some neat parts.

lar practice, but it fits the point we are making here. Traditionally, we'd be looking at a lengthy procedure where several cuts would be made to the side of the fender from the edge to the top of the side. These cuts, a dozen or more depending on the length of the fender, would give relief to the fender, as a strap would pull it tight to the wheel, thus correcting the radius and matching that of the wheel.

Another pretty common thing to do to a flat strap fender is to weld on some round stock to add to the strength of it and to make it a little more custom. With a basic understanding of welding here, this is an easy job with great results.

Today we have the luxury through shops like Bare Knuckle Choppers to learn about things like the shrinker/stretcher tools often used for this work. This tool, with opposing jaws, can take a straight piece of metal, 18-gauge mild steel, 20-gauge stainless, or 16-gauge aluminum, and bend it into a smooth radius. By multiplying the amount of force on the jaws 45 to 1, you can effortlessly shrink or stretch the radius in your steel fender. Since it changes the metal on a molecular level, the edges can be smoothed out with a dolly and hammer without very much loss in the adjusted radius.

Additionally, in either case mentioned above, an English wheel should be used over the top of the fender once the radius has been adjusted. An English wheel is a tool of the trade dating back to the 1900s when men called "panel beaters" were making body panels out of flat steel. The tool is comprised of a large upper wheel and a series of smaller, interchangeable wheels called anvils, both mounted on opposing sides of a giant c-shaped stand. The lower wheel is raised into position providing pressure against the sheet metal and the top wheel. As the metal rides across the two rollers, a yoke at the bottom can increase or decrease pressure to achieve the desired effect. I honestly wish I could tell you more about it but mastering this tool takes years. For our purpose, a few passes will smooth out any small creases that may have been incurred during our shrinking of the radius.

Hand Fabbed Sheet Metal:

Building your own sheet metal from scratch will give you a level of pride like nothing you've ever achieved, but it takes a long time to acquire the skills needed to perform fabrication of this level. In the case where you've been at it a while and are ready to start trying your hand at the craft, then we can suggest some tools and instruction to that end.

The Eastwood Company makes a nice selection of tools for sheet metal fabrication; the first of which you should invest in is a good hammer and dolly set. They have one for about a hundred bucks and even the lightest level of sheet metal work will require these tools.

Even simple tricks can help you take a store bought part and make it shine.

Your tank is like the face of a bike. Choosing the right one is crucial. If it looks wrong, be honest and swap it out early.

Lemme shows the results of smoothing out the weld with an English Wheel and a belt sander.

Use of the English Wheel dates back to the 1900's when they still called sheet metal fabricators "Pannel Beaters."

The heat from the weld can help you bend a rod around the lip of a fender. Do it an inch or so at a time to make this simple.

There is nothing that will look as good as a fender made from scratch for your bike, but that skill takes time to master.

A good tool like this shrinker can save hours of cutting and welding.

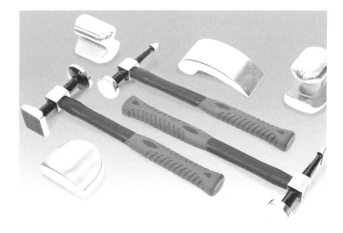

Having the right tool for the job is an understatement when it comes to sheet metal fabrication.

Eastwood

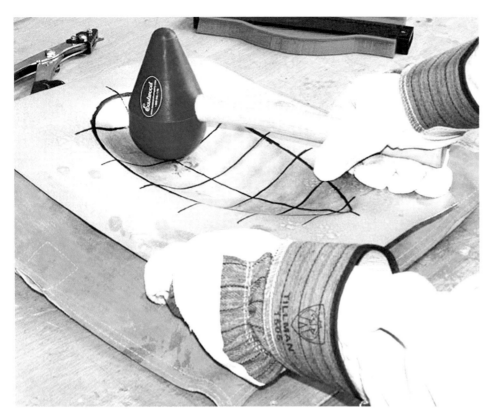

Eastwood has an extensive selection of these specialty tools. www.eastwood.com/

Eastwood also offers every expert level metal fabrication tool you can imagine, from planishing hammers to panel beater mallets and sandbags. They also have an entire library on how to do everything with sheet metal. Having used some of their self-help tech media myself, I can recommend them comfortably.

The very publisher that has brought you this book has a complete line-up in the "how to" section of metal fabrication including: *Sheet Metal Bible.* This book is filled with legendary fabricators like Ron Covell, Craig Naff, Rob Roehl and Bruce Terry. The projects inside are for hot rods and choppers so you can't go wrong. The point is, if you want to continue from the beginner level of this art, the information is out there just waiting for you. Enjoy!

Here is another book from Wolfgang Publications that will guide you through a better understanding of sheet metal fab.

43

7
ALL ABOUT MOUNTS

One of the many details you will have to figure out during your new build will be the mounts. You'll have dozens of mounts on your bike for dozens of components. While the size is tiny, the importance is not. It is quite easy to breeze through your build with your eyes on the prize, all the while neglecting the quality and strength of your mounts. Rest assured, this will cause much frustration in the future. We all know how much vibration the V-twin engine generates, and the added stresses of the road, kick starting, weather, etc, all contribute to a need for sturdy mounts throughout your build. Take the time to learn and understand a few simple guidelines for the many mounts on your bike.

Solid Mount vs. Rubber Mount

There are literally hundreds of different styles of mounts, but they all breakdown into two separate categories: solid or rubber mount. The respective titles pretty much say everything. Each individual component calls for its own considerations when deciding whether to use a rubber mount or a solid mount. You cannot decide to rubber mount everything on your bike, nor can each piece be solid mounted. There are a few important factors that will help you decide to rubber mount or solid mount.

Solid mounts will always be the most common mounts on a custom bike. Ideally your build will be one solid piece everywhere your body contacts the bike. The seat, while of course carrying the cushion it may have, will be bolted firmly to your frame, or possibly held in place with a hinge and springs. Your controls will be bolted solidly to the frame. Your grips tightly fastened to the bars (while the bars may be rubber mounted to your trees). This allows you to feel your bike as you navigate the streets. If any of this was rubber mounted, your feel, and subsequently your reactions, would be mushy and sluggish.

Additionally, all of your small and medium sized components will be solid mounted, with rare exception. Sissybars, fenders, exhaust pipes, taillights, controls, kickstands, should all be mounted directly to the frame or other mounting location. Brakes are ALWAYS solid mounted. While there are numerous types of "floating" mounts, rubber will rarely, if ever, be involved. It will never be an isolation style mount.

For the most part, if the component you are mounting contains a considerable amount of fluid, i.e. gas and oil tanks, rubber mounting is most likely the best option. While there are other parts on your bike that are of comparable size and shape, your tanks carry a completely different set of features that require rubber mounting. Fluid is constantly moving, shifting, and vibrating while the bike is running. Also, the material carrying the fluid is likely thinner than other materials on the bike. This means that your gas and oil tank mounts will benefit from the vibration isolation that a quality rubber mount

offers. There are a few different types of rubber mounts, but the basic idea involves the two pieces to be fastened together, a fastener, and a rubber isolator between the two pieces. The fastener passes through each piece as well as the rubber, and as the fastener is tightened, the rubber expands and forms a taught fit around the pieces. Now the mounted component will stay securely fastened to the bike, but the vibration transferred to the piece will be greatly reduced.

Rubber Mounts

A very versatile type of mount is the "flat-side gas tank" mount. These are available as a kit from quality, independent motorcycle shops. These provide you with a rubber isolator and a steel insert. You will need to source your own fastener. The steel insert allows the fastener and base to pull tight together, and the rubber keeps the mounted component and the base from contacting one another. These are available in many shapes and sizes.

Bare Knuckle Chopper's custom bike "Incognegro" show here is a great example of using custom mounts like a pro.

A three piece rubber mount is a common type of mount in the industry today.

I prefer to use the variety that requires a ¼ inch mount thickness and a 13/16 inch hole. These allow for the use of a 5/16 inch fastener.

If you want to go a little further into the custom world, you can fashion your own isolation mounts. There are many outlets to find rubber, foam rubber, or leather to suit your style and needs. In many cases I will use leather between a small gas tank and the frame mounts. I always build my tanks with excessively strong mounts, so my fear of cracking is reduced. I do, however, wish to protect the paint and reduce some vibration.

Solid Mounts

You are really unlimited in your choice of solid mounts. If the situation calls for a solid mount, you really need to be sure your material thickness and quality are substantial, choose a sufficient size and grade fastener, and make your mount. You can really be creative here. One of my favorite styles of mount is the spud and biscuit style. The spud uses a through hole and a recessed shoulder for an

Here the rubber mount is shown being used as a gas tank mount along the back bone of the frame.

In this pic you can see the same mount being used to mount an oil tank to the frame rail.

Allen or 12 point bolt, and the biscuit is threaded. The biscuit should have a shoulder so the smaller I.D. fits in a hole smaller than the shoulder. This allows for two things: you have a little room to move the biscuit around for perfect alignment, and, more importantly, the increased surface area over the smaller hole will reduce the tendency for cracking or tearing around the mount.

A simple tab style mount goes a long way as well. These are handy in many circumstances, such as mounting seats, master cylinders, taillights, even exhaust pipes. Again, be sure your material is of sufficient thickness, and be sure your fasteners are fit to the task, and get creative. Some pieces may call for a slotted hole to allow for adjustment, as an exhaust pipe often will. You can machine this, or drill two holes at the length of your desired adjustment, and connect the holes with a cutoff wheel or die grinder.

You've got to find a place to hang your switches, too. This again, is limited only by your imagination. The thickness of your mount can be thinner for switch plates, but don't go too light. You can find many outlets for ready made switch mounts, or you can make your own. The key here is placement, and a good, quality weld. Easy.

Major Component Mounts

There are a few parts of the bike where you must get mounts dead on right. If you aren't confident that your craftsmanship, or welding is sufficient for these important mounts, seek the advice of a professional.

There are numerous styles of brake caliper mounts, but all demand a few simple requirements. Your caliper must always be in alignment, the mount has to be made of sufficiently strong material, the fasteners should be Grade 8 (minimum) and weld quality must be very good. It must be secured in a fashion that will never allow binding, and the fasteners must never come loose. This sounds simple enough, but never cut corners here. Many a bike has been destroyed by lackadaisical brake mounting.

Isolation mounts are a great way to mount a gas tank and can be made with leather or foam rubber or foam washers.

This is a great shot of a spud and biscuit style solid mount.

Here you can see same spud and biscuit being used to mount a strut to a fender.

A tab style mount is a nice simple mount that only requires good placement and a good weld.

This is an example of a good switch plate mount.

Major component mounts can sound simple but in truth must be handled with exacting precision.

Fenders are a tricky mount, because you have a lot going on. Always be sure your drivetrain is completely aligned and bolted down in what will be the final position. This includes rear wheel and chain. Make sure when mocking up the fender, your tire is fully inflated. Center the wheel and tire, and mount your brake. Then double check everything. Now you are ready to mount your fender. When considering fender mounts, you must consider a few details. Will you be carrying a passenger? Do you intend to run a sissybar or struts? Will there be any other weight the fender must carry? These considerations all dictate size and shape of your fender mounts. I like to incorporate at least three mounting locations for the fender: bottom, middle and top. I usually run a low mount from the bottom to the transmission area, then one from the middle to the seat area, and then a strut or sissybar. This changes if I run a short fender, as I will then only run the middle and top mounts.

There are literally hundreds of ways to mount your oil tank, but I try to stick to a basic system. I really like using the flatside gas tank mounts for my oil tanks. Two simple tabs from the top and one from the rear provides ample strength for your oil bag.

Gas tank mounting is where you make yourself a hero or a complete zero. Isolation mounting of some sort is always recommended, but you can go about it many different ways. For larger tanks I like to use the flatside mounts from the backbone, and inserts in the bottom of the tank. For smaller tanks I often use leather or a rubber biscuit under the tank on top of the backbone.

Fasteners

Now that your bike is back from paint, you are ready to start bolting the beauty back together. But those bolts you scrounged for mock-up are not going to cut it. They are ugly, and simply not up to snuff. When choosing fasteners you must keep in mind a 'theme' throughout the bike, meaning do not mix stainless steel with chrome, 12 point with Allen head, Nylock with lock washers. Of course function must precede form in this instance, so do not compromise integrity for the sake of looking good. All of your fasteners must be held in place by more than just a good twist of the wrench. Apply recommended torque values where applicable. Use thread-locker or another locking device of some sort. I prefer lock washers, as you can check them and retighten them on the road. If threadlock breaks loose, it is done; you must clean the fastener and reapply. Nylocks are intended for one time use. A quality lock washer should insure tightness for years.

As for the particular type of fastener, that is up to you. I prefer 12 point stainless steel fasteners, such as those offered by ARP. Hex heads and Allen heads are also acceptable. I try to stay away from button heads as much as possible, as the smaller Allen drives on button heads tend to strip easily. No matter the style you choose, be sure they are quality. And if you choose to run a threadlocker, ALWAYS clean the chrome from the fastener, as the threadlock will not adhere to chrome.

This is a great shot of a strong solid fender mount in the middle location.

Strength is the major consideration in mounting oil tanks. Remember that, grade for grade, stainless fasteners are not as strong as steel.

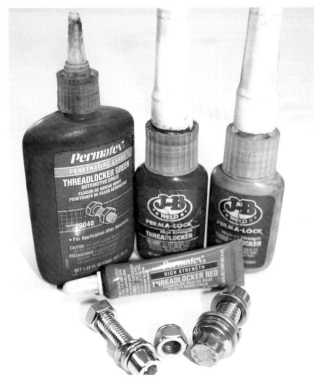

The right loc-tite for mounting hardware is crucial. If you're not sure, ask someone.

Here is a nice tight close up of a gas tank mount using leather biscuits to isolate the tank.

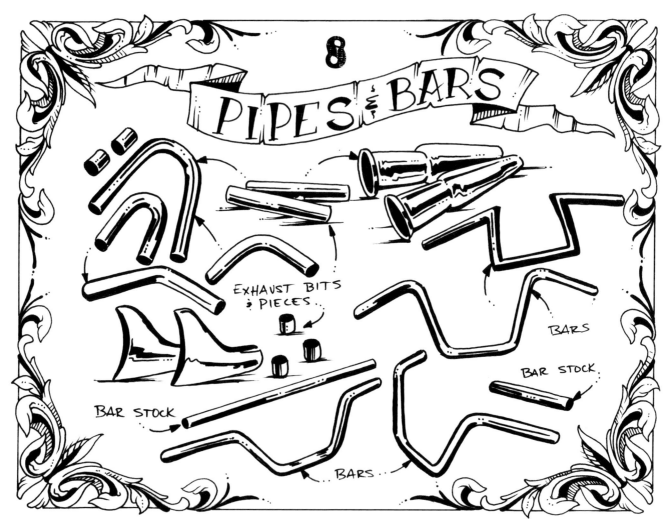

8
PIPES & BARS

EXHAUST BITS & PIECES

BARS

BAR STOCK

BAR STOCK

BAR STOCK

BARS

In the beginning stages of learning to customize your motorcycle, some of the easiest items to tackle are the pipes and bars. With these two components alone you can drastically change the personality of a bike. In the aftermarket today there are like a million different options. Taking some of the parts available in the catalogues and making them into your own can be easy enough, with the right tools and practice.

How About The Pipes:

I know by now you've undoubtedly had your grubby little grabbers on a few catalogues and have seen the massive section that most of them have for exhaust systems, mufflers and builders' kits. Well, this section is to assure you that just because the parts supplier has a certain type of exhaust for a specific model, that doesn't have to limit your choices. It's a very popular proposition today to swap applications and end up with exotic combinations like standard head pipes with a sport bike muffler. Another option can be a complete system built from one of the many builders' kits available today. We're going to show you an example of the last option just to get you started because learning to work with bends can free you up to use almost anything from any bike for your exhaust.

With the economy as tough as it is, not everyone can afford a thousand-dollar exhaust system. Skull Headers, Jeggs, Summit and Paughco all offer builder kits and tubing like this. You can select different types of tubing; in this example we are using 1-1/4 inch stock. When you buy the tubing in a kit from a motorcycle supplier it will let you select the application and get two head tubes for what you are building, i.e.: Panhead, Shovel, etc.

So let's start off by considering that you already have your mounts for mufflers figured out, if you're using mufflers. Using the builder's kit you begin by marking a cut line.

Ideally you will want to use a band saw to make your cuts, but even if you are using a cut off wheel, you must always make your cuts perpendicular, whether it's a straight piece or on a bend. If you do not do this, the diameter of the pipe will change and it will become impossible to weld it to the other pipes.

You can go back and forth from the bike to the band saw as often as you want to get the perfect fit. Just remember, before you weld the section into place, clean up the edges with a belt sander to remove the burrs or imperfections.

As each piece gets tack welded into place, you'll see the pipes starting to take shape. Remember, take your time and think about your options, how you

The right bars can make a bike look perfect and ride like a dream.

As far as the look goes, placement of the pipes can be as important as the type of pipe itself.

Here is an example of Paughco's builder kit for making your own exhaust system.

want the pipes to look and pay attention to anything that might get in the way during the final assembly.

Once you have everything tacked in place and you're sure of what you have mocked-up on the bike, you can move on to final welding. You will do well to take your time on these steps, so weld slowly and in as small an area as possible. Keep a body hammer with you so you can tap the edges to keep them close and the weld tight.

With the welding done, it's time to finish the surface. Starting with a 60 grit flapper disc, work the surface of the weld down just to the point that it reaches the surface of the pipe. Careful here, it goes fast.

From there you work outward from the center of the weld an inch or so using a die grinder with Rol-Loc sanding discs to feather the edge of the weld with the metal of the pipe.

Finally, using a DA sander with 80 grit paper, work out an additional two inches to further feather the edge, leaving an unnoticeable seam. A once-over with lighter grades of sandpaper can get it ready for finishing.

While chrome is an awesome finish for pipes, it takes much more surface prep, going up in grades of sandpaper with the DA to a 320 or better. It also requires finish welding to fill in any abnormalities. This is one of the reasons pipe wrap, that can be purchased from companies like DEI, is very popular today. With a treatment of heat paint, then a layer of pipe wrap, you're done.

These pieces can be cut to different lengths to fit your need.

A good band saw can make this work so much easier, but it can be done without one.

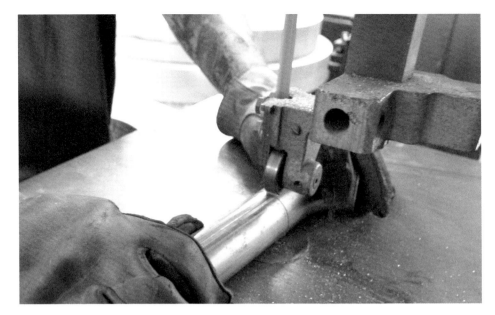

A belt sander will help you take the ends down slowly and get the best fit.

Keep in mind all moving components that might get obstructed by the placement of the exhaust.

Slow easy welding is important here and will help you get a good finish.

Here you see Paul using the flapper disc on an electric grinder. Remember to go slow.

For the tight spots he switches to the angle grinder with a 2 inch disc.

Behind The Bars:

Today there are plenty of bars to choose from. It seems as if everyone who builds bikes in fact has a collection of custom bars. So choosing a set is not that hard, in order to get a great look for your custom bike. Oh sure, making a pair is way better if you have the skills, and it's not like this would be beyond the scope of good reason or ability, even for a beginner. Consider my ol' man and some of his friends who bent their bars back in the day with a conduit tubing bender; things have come a long way.

Sticking to some guidelines can help you make sure that your bars will be safe and come out the way you want them to. First, you should always stick with tubing that is DOM and it's best to stick with .095 wall. If you end up using an internal throttle the diameter will be .800 so you will be all set up for it. The reason for the DOM tubing is that seam welded tubing will have a flat spot and look bad no matter what finish you put over it. The last thing you want are a pair of bars that break while you're ass deep in a wild ride. Another thing to remember is that welding bars together takes a similar sized material to allow for the natural flexion that the bars would have if they were bent from a single piece of tubing.

There will be times that you will have to employ the skills you have been learning in the other steps of metal working, even if you choose a set of pre-made bars. Take for instance my six bends for the Pan. They were a great set of bars from Paughco but I didn't want to use dog bone risers that tipped in so I ordered straight ones and hoped the bars would be wide enough to accommodate them. It turned out that they were an inch and a half shy of the width that I needed. Now I could have given in on the risers and just ordered a set that would fit better. Instead, I cut, trim and welded up the new bars.

In the end he will go over the weld areas with coarse sand paper on an orbital sander then switch to lighter grades as he moves out further away from the weld.

Pipe wrap like the stuff you can get from DEI is widely popular today and a quick finish trick.

For this style of bike I knew from the beginning that six bend bars would be a perfect fit.

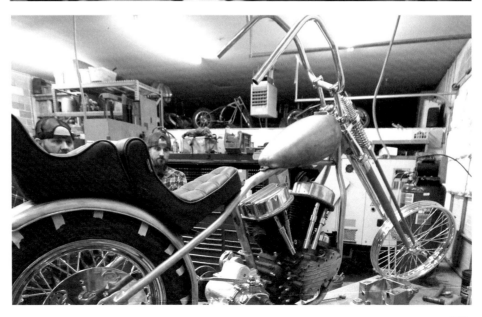

They would need considerable adjusting to actually be that perfect fit in the end.

With much of the same technique used in finishing your pipes, you can make the bar modifications almost unnoticeable. Again, take your time and remember taking more off a little at a time is so much easier than starting all over because you were too aggressive with the grinder.

There are a million other things we could talk about in this chapter, but like the title of the book says, these are the basics and this should be enough information to get you started. Asking advice along the way will take you far but the courage to forge ahead on your own will develop the essential skills to work around anything you run into.

This was mainly because I had to have the damn dog bone risers to go with them.

When adding to the width remember the slug should be an identical wall thickness to ensure the same flexibility.

Unfortunately, there is no short cut for a trip back to the chrome or paint shop at this point.

Trampin' Is Back In Style

Remember when we were kids how cool it used to be to sleep outside? Even when it was just in the backyard, the feeling you got from doing your own thing was a blast. Over the years though, whether from the increasing belief that we were too old or that we deserved better, we somehow walked away from these juvenile tendencies to rough it.

Now I know that you have identified this metamorphosis as well as I have. You know the guys that pull up in the billion dollar Winnebagos or better yet, the cats who just have a "must stay in a hotel" rule about traveling. Somewhere we have, in part, moved away from the basic "let's just split" mentality that has made the word biker mean more than just a person who rides a motorcycle.

Today, this is starting to change however. I'm not sure if it is the result of a slow economy, the rising price of gas, the cost of attending a national event for a week, or just the plain old need to reconnect with Mutha Nature, but people are rejoining their inner child and that sense of being okay with sleeping outside. And this doesn't mean that you have to take out a loan to do it man, just ride the bike, sleep where you may, eat when you can and let God handle the rest.

I have seen little boys, with the attitudes young men often have, come home all grown up, just from a trip across the country where everything wasn't provided for before they left. You could see a proud look in their eyes that they got from knowing they accomplished more than driving from one state to another; they had survived road tripping like a true scooter tramp. Sleeping under picnic tables, showering at truck stops, eating a continental breakfast at a hotel you didn't stay at, all might seem like living less to the norms of society, but for a few of us, it's pure heaven. Today, the life of a tramp is still something you can't buy over the counter, and I'm so glad to see it coming back in style.

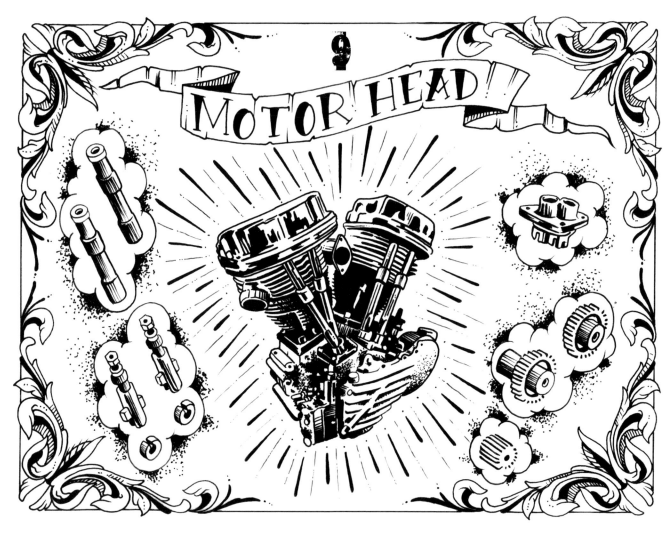

here are so many options for a builder to take when it comes to which motor to use, or even where to start. What this chapter intends to do is not only give you a few of these options, as it will, but more importantly, it will give you a brief look into the time honored tradition of rehabbing old iron.

Buying New:

First and foremost, you have to give it up to S&S for pushing this thing as far to the edge of the performance envelope as they have. They have also made it possible for those of us who didn't get the chance to own a Pan or a Knuckle back in the day, an opportunity to have one today through their Flathead Power line of powerplants.

Swap Meet Mill:

While there is nothing wrong at all with the price point of a swap meet engine, but it is for sure a situation of buyer beware. Unless you know what you're looking at, this can be a bad risk to take with your budget as it can get costly fast. This is a good time to find someone with experience to take along to the meet.

Rehab Not For Quitters:

In the world of custom motorcycle building today, the likelihood that you will be rebuilding, or having someone rebuild an engine for you, is pretty good. In the pursuit of building my '49 I had the great honor of spending a week with a legend in this arena. His name is Shelton Davis, the 73 year old father of my brother Roadside. Mr. Davis, or the "Godfather" as his friends and brothers call him, has been at this for some 40 years and agreed to have me at his shop for a week to learn how to build a Pan. While this will NOT be a step-by-step to that end, I thought it was important to show you exactly what kind of tools and knowledge it takes. He is pictured here going over the '49 cases and extracting all the broken hardware; I think it was five bolts to start with.

After Mr. Davis cleaned away 60 years of abuse, Roadside took me to Easy's place and we started by sandblasting everything: cases, heads, flywheels and cylinders. Back at the shop, they all got cleaned and inspected.

We started in a little side room of the shop. A place had been cleared at the bench where hundreds of other motors had been built. We heated the cases and removed the old main bearing races, installed new races and set the two case halves together.

This was when I learned about making ice cream. In order to get new bearings and races to fit properly, you have to line ream or lap the races. One side at a time, you run this hand crank line reamer for about ten minutes per side, not going too fast so as to create heat, and stopping often to clean and check the clearances. It took me some four hours to get this to a good fit before we moved on. Trust me, better a little extra time here than a loose lower end from going too fast.

We used old flywheels with a new crank, pinion and sprocket shaft. Mr. Davis pulled out his collection of flywheel hardware and I found myself wishing I could hear all the stories from the bikes these parts had been on. He immediately spotted the right components for this model and went to work.

Building or rebuilding a motor for your project is another art form of an accomplished craftsmen.

S&S offers some great options that make it easy for a less experienced builder to have a reliable old school engine.

Just because it looks like a whole motor doesn't actually mean it will require less work.

Everything needs to be cleaned, sand blasted and inspected at the start.

A grey beard that's been doing motor builds for years is still the best resource there is.

As we tapped the old races out, I think my heart skipped a beat. One mistake here and your cases are junk.

With the flywheels assembled, we set them into the truing stand, and a few spins later Shelton located the areas on each side where a little persuasion was needed.

With the flywheels out of the stand, he showed me those areas, and using a brass hammer I brought a swift blow to the face of each wheel. This went on for a good 20 minutes back and forth until we were within a thousandth.

Roadside loaded the assembly into the one case half then put the lid on it so we could stand it up and check for sprocket shaft endplay.

On these older motors the process for fitting the bearings to the races takes hours.

Only a soft metal hammer can be used on the flywheels for adjusting their position.

A lifetime collection of hardware is a huge advantage here as well.

Here we measure the sprocket shaft end play.

The truing stand is another must have tool for this work and will coast a good bit, but you have to have one.

You will need to have the cylinders honed, possibly bored out to a larger size, if you are reworking the top end.

Everything must be checked for clearance when assembling the motor.

Although it looks ominous, the cam chest on the Panhead is not too complicated when you assemble everything a step at a time.

With both halves of the case on, we installed a tool on the sprocket side that gave us the exact measurement of the shim we would need for proper clearance. Then we pulled the right shim out of a pile and installed it. After that, we bolted everything together for good, with some seam sealer on the surfaces where the cases come together.

With our lower end assembled, we took a quick ride over to CP Cylinder Head and Machine where they knocked our used cylinders out to 50-over and fit them to the new pistons we had ordered in.

The next morning at the shop, we had one more step to go before we could get into the top end. The cam chest was empty. After getting the right wheels and gears in place to drive the new oil pump Roadside had installed, his dad measured for cam endplay. We installed the proper shim and closed up the cam case.

Looking at the internals of a Panhead motor makes you appreciate how special they are. Finding a cam chest cover for a '49 Panhead really made me appreciate this even more as the one I had scored was wrong, no matter what Roadside and I were told.

Once we had both pistons fitted with new rings and installed on the rods, we were

Piston ring pliers will help get the cylinders over the pistons.

Using old parts like these pan heads can take a huge amount of rehab work to make them ready to install.

ready to get the freshly painted cylinders into place. New gaskets with top secret sealer, then a ring compressor and the cylinders slid on like hot butter.

We were starting with a beautifully matched set of heads that Shelton pulled from his collection for me. The heads I planned to use were two different sizes and hadn't been updated for a rubber-band manifold like these; it was a big head start. They would still need several studs replaced, threads cleaned, etc. before being dropped on to the '49.

In another room sat the bench where Mr. Davis did his head work. We heated the heads and tapped out the old valve guides then installed new ones. This whole process is an art in itself that would take a lifetime to master.

Using a Black & Decker electric valve grinder and stones, he slicked up the valve seats then installed new valves and finish lapped them back on the bench.

With new springs, seals and collars on all the valves, we installed the rockers and put on the trademark Pan lids. This was made easier in two parts. First, Roadside cleaned every tiny thread so they would be secured correctly and evenly. And secondly, from grabbing the tins we were having a hard time with "and wallowing out the holes." Funny how you can overlook simple things when you're trying to be so careful, huh?

After both heads were secured, Roadside worked on the intake ports so the manifold fit perfectly. You can stand on this one and it isn't going anywhere.

As we installed the pushrods and tubes, I realized what an incredible five days it had been since I showed up at this shop, a thousand miles from home. Roadside's father had taken us on the field trip of our lives and shown us how to take life by the horns and get it done. Now I know that this hardly served as a complete guide to building your

Over his shoulder you can see Shelton has everything he needs for doing head work within arms reach.

Each step we took in making the old heads new again got me more fired up to bolt them on. I could hear it running by this point.

At this stage they almost look like new castings fresh out of the box.

Pan, but it wasn't meant to. In fact there were several steps left out. What I hope you get from this chapter is the idea that there are parts of this thing that you simply cannot buy, like the traditions that have been passed down from father to son for generations. If you're willing and patient, someone will be there to teach you. If you want to just run around with a fist full of money, there'll be someone there to help with that too, but you'll probably get a lot less out of the project that way.

Now I realize that for me to truly build a motor like this on my own I will need a couple thousand-dollars in tools and a few years to get it all right, but that's the point. It's not something you just decide to start doing and poof, you have it. What Roadside and I gained that week was the confidence to go after this stuff on our own next time. It was a gift that I will treasure for the rest of my life.

Here is a shot of the updated intake that we switched from the old plumber style.

There are few things as rewarding as building a motor from the bottom up.

Teach A Man to Fish

You've probably all heard this ancient Chinese proverb: Give a man a fish, and you feed him for a day. Teach a man to fish, and you feed him for a lifetime. Now I had known these words for more than half my life, but it was in a little motorcycle shop just outside of Pensacola, Florida this past month that I got a true appreciation for that quote.

There in a small shop outside of my brother Roadisde's hometown, his father, 73 year old Shelton Davis, was going to teach me how to build a Pan. Now at this point I was blown away, I mean this cat is a legend in and out of his area and just to get the chance to work with him would have been enough. What I ended up learning during my time in Florida was that Shelton, for both our benefits, was teaching us how to fish, in a manner of speaking.

As we prepped each piece, I began to realize what it was I was taking part in: the tried and true methods of making old iron new again. This was so much better to me than if I would have had the dough to just buy this motor from someone who had done all the work.

I was a page right out of the "Metaphysics of Motorcycling." With 40 years of experience behind him, he sat there like my grandfather used to and made me use my hands to bring this thing to life. He explained how and why things worked in the motor and we told stories all the while from his past and my own. At that moment, we were not an older and younger man, not a rebel or a Yankee. No, we were nothing more than two tramps digging on the trip of resurrecting an old Pan.

What I left with from Shelton's shop was not just a glorious tribute to Harley's days gone by, but with the confidence to build a Pan again on my own. Now it might take me a lifetime to be anywhere near the craftsman that Mr. Davis is, but what I do know is that from this day on, I will never go hungry again because he taught me how to fish.

So you've toiled away at your precious little gem for months, maybe years now, and you've reached the point that it is a solid mock-up, the driveline, sheet metal and various other adornments are on and in proper order. Now it's time to send all the pieces out for their perspective coatings and finishes. Stop, right there! Do not more forward in a hasty manner and think that by hauling ass through the fifteen minutes that it could possibly be done in that you will somehow get your parts back faster. Do not believe for one minute, unless you have done this for years and are able to identify a set of transmission mounting bolts from across the room, that you will be able to figure everything out when the parts come back. By taking your time here, compartmentalizing your hardware and mounts as they come off the bike, you will save aggravation later and you will be prepared to occupy yourself while you wait for paint. Before we get into the busy time stuff, let's take a look at some healthy practices that can help you stay on track.

Bag it:

It may seem trivial but putting your hardware in little plastic bags with an identifying tag as to where they belong on the motorcycle can do wonders for the final assembly. By keeping the specific hardware at the ready and separated, not only will it go faster, you will have an opportunity to go over each of the bags and see if any of the hardware you have is not up to snuff.

Wrap it:

There will be several parts that come off the bike that are already chrome or finished. In order to keep from taking any steps backward, it may be a good idea to wrap these parts in an old towel and put them up on a shelf. Remember the shelves from Chapter One?

The Busy Work:

So the paint is out, the chrome is in the shop and the table where you were building your bike is now empty; what should you do next? One thing is for sure, as I know all too well going through this as I write, builder withdrawal will set in. You see, the fevered tempo that will undoubtedly ensue during the final stages of mock-up gets you so amped up that you are left with an overloading surplus of kinetic energy while you sit and wait for the next stage. This is a perfect time for busy work that will make the final assembly a breeze.

Swap It:

The hardware that you had bagged up, at the same time you are inspecting it for damaged goods, you may well realize that it would be better back in the bin to be used for future mock-ups. In its place you can put nice chrome or stainless goodies and by taking your bags to the local ironmonger, they will be easy to swap out. In my case, the cats at Cycle Warehouse have a real sweet set of Gardner Westcott stuff that I have access to so I picked out some upgrades for the '49. If you are happy with your existing hardware, take

Take your time during tear down and you will be better prepared for final assembly.

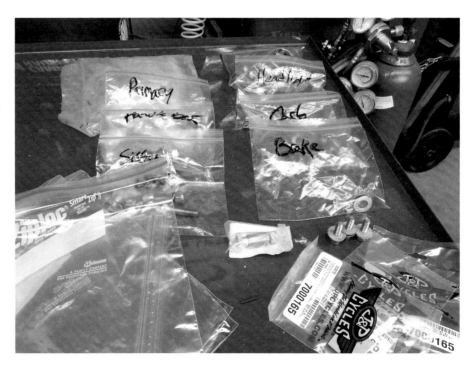

Ziploc has a great solution to keep you organized during tear down.

Protecting chrome and painted parts while you are between steps can save big.

You have time, get critical and clean it up with some better hardware.

The hand made polishing wheel from chapter one in action.

God Matt is a brave soul here right? And neither one of us has the brains to wear gloves here....... Hmmmm

some time to see if you need to chase any of the threads: clean them up with a tap and die set.

Polish It:

This idle time is also great for taking things that could use a good polish and get them lined up. I grabbed a professional polishing kit from Eastwood and went to it with my SU carb. Roadside hooked me up with this thing like a year ago and I hung it on the wall, never thinking twice about it while the build was going on. Once I tore into it and got the body disassembled for a quick rebuild, I decided to spend some time giving it some bling. I didn't want to send this out for chrome because eventually I might engrave some cool stuff on it so for now a high polish of the aluminum is good enough.

Clean It:

There will be plenty of parts that need cleaning in a manner similar to the ones that are getting polished even if cleaning them is all the further you intend to go. Some of the used parts I am bolting on the Pan, like the clutch assembly and pressure plate, needed to be gone over to make sure they would make the cut and be in good working order for the final assembly. This also gives you time to closely examine any used parts while there is no rush, so that if you need to replace something, it can be ordered in plenty of time.

Inventory It:

Oh yeah, back to your list from Chapter Two. Even though you got the bike mocked-up and all the necessary items were prepped and assembled for sending out to paint, there will still quite likely be unfinished pieces. This is a good time to go over your list or add to it with all the unfinished work and take a look at your inventory. Are all the parts you need on hand or do you still have things that need to be ordered in? By staying in touch with your painter and asking for progress reports and a real timeline, you will know when the deadline will be to make sure it's all on hand.

Clean It:

No, I'm not repeating myself. This time the "clean it" refers to the shop or space you're building in. Unless you're suffering from obsessive-compulsive disorder, the final stages of the mock-up are liable to leave your space in a wreck. This is a good time to get the clutter under control, clean and put away all the tools and get ready for another round of insanity because when that painted frame hits the front door, it's on!

Stock It:

And speaking of the shop, this is also a good time to make sure you have everything on hand as far as shop supplies. This may be time to add to the list again. Think about the things you will need and check your provision for: Loc-tite, anti-seize, brake and carb cleaner, dielectric grease, wire, terminal ends, three-in-one oil, clean shop rags, bearing grease, electric tape, low adhesive tape, plumbing tape, solder, wire ties, steel wire, oil,

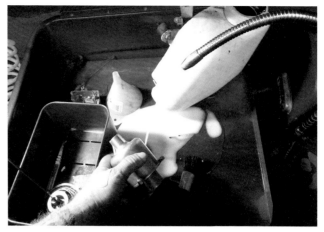

The last thing you will want in final assembly is to work with dirty parts.

That black peg board pays off now with line of sight inventory of where your stuff is.

Getting your shop in order to make ready for the final build is essential.

Stocking up on shop products will save your ass in the late hours when everything is closed.

Albert and Mailman shown here sharing stories from the old days and bikes they built along the way.

gas, spray cleaner and polish. I know that went on a little bit, but I wanted to make the point that you should think your way through the rest of the build. Try to have everything on hand that might be required to go out the back door without stopping.

Talk About It:

Now this might seem like an unnecessary step, but I found that talking to other throttle junkies can serve more than just the purpose of keeping your mind off of the fact that in nine days, three hours, twenty-two minutes and six seconds your paint will be back. It also reminds you of overlooked steps. Good friends who have built custom bikes themselves can be a wealth of information and most of them, at least as sick as you at this point, will think nothing of an hour-long conversations of what you are building.

Build It:

In closing Chapter Nine, I just want to mention that you should take your time when you begin final assembly. An extra day or two added to the months or years you have been building this bike will be worth it when compared to the time you will lose if you drop the tank on the floor, strip a thread or bust a part that you would have to reorder. It's been a long road to this point so just take your time and enjoy the ride.

Putting all the parts within arms reach, just like Roadside's dad had stuff positioned, is a good place to start.

Passing The Torch

"It used to be that the man who rode these bikes made the machine what it was. Today, more commonly, it's the machine that makes the man." This was a quote made by a good friend of mine and although I understood what he meant when he first laid it on me, it wasn't until years later when I found myself using his quote in conversation that I really understood its meaning. It prompted me to think about a time when motorcycling wasn't as popular as it is today, people who rode were often outcasts as far as society was concerned, but motorcycles, man, motorcycles were just cool!

Before I go any further, let me try to clarify what exactly I mean about the time when motorcycles were cool. Like my friend had illustrated in his quote, it was the type of rugged individualist who could be found on the motorcycle which gave it such mystique. This was partially due to the overwhelming commitment it took to be a biker in those days. You had to know your bike to keep it on the road. To get this knowledge, if you weren't already mechanically inclined, you had to find the guys that did know and pay your dues. In those days, bikes at the average cycle meet were as varied as the people. The bikes had great big Springer and girder frontends, giant sissybars and there was almost never a bike that didn't have a seat for your lady.

I do have a light at the end of the tunnel: there is a new generation coming into this thing we all dig and man, they have their own way of doing things. Whatever the motivation, they're making a decision to live it, to ride the bike, to make friendships that will last a lifetime, and to challenge themselves and the machines they ride. They are doing all the things that we are now sitting around campfires telling stories about, and after all, those are the times we remember. As long as there are stories about sleeping in a ditch overnight, or warming up under the hand dryer at a rest stop and sharing a bag of chips when we were riding home too broke to buy food, they will be the things we remember.

THE PAINT BOOTH

11

For most of us, it's not easy picturing something physically finished inside the limits of the mind, but painters are a rare breed: good ones, anyway. I can't even begin to talk about the plethora of options you have concerning paint, but I can say that if you really need your scoot to shine with flawless perfection, there are only a handful of artists out there who can accomplish that task, and *artists* is an understatement here.

It seems that almost everybody knows somebody else who grasps the concept of adhering chemicals to steel, but that's a far cry from a strategically arranged masterpiece with a mirror finish. And since Chris has had about thirty some odd years to dream up this Pan, there was no way he was just going to leave the fate of its skin up to just anybody with an air compressor and a paint gun.

Enter Jeremy Peterson, owner of Relic Customs in Austin, Minnesota. He is one of these multi-talented freaks with an almost obsessive eye for detail, and he is able to wrap the vicious personality of a good death machine in such an amazing coat of beauty that even the most fearful would be left begging for a ride. Needless to say, Chris chose well leaving the fate of his Pan's exterior in the hands of Jeremy.

It goes without saying that when it comes to choosing a design and color, the options are endless. Even some of the most seasoned painters couldn't lay down such a design as this. Not as good anyway. So in this chapter, I'll walk you through the daunting task Jeremy had set before him and try to explain to you the steps he took as we go. Despite the way he makes it look easy, hang on tight, 'cause it's a mind-bending journey from steel to shine that you won't want to miss, and here we go.

In most cases, if you stop by on a sunny day, when the temperature is just right and the wind isn't too strong or the barometric pressure isn't too low, you'll probably find Jeremy's brother Nick out in the shop lending a hand to any of their creations. Nearby we see Nick doing some final bodywork on Chris's Pan. We can only assume that Jeremy "let" Nick do this because of the wild amounts of fun it truly is. (Insert sarcastic eye-roll here.)

Daniel Donnley stayed at my house for a week while we built "Ticket To Ride."

Despite the monotonous and terribly painful nature of bodywork, it is imperative that you take your time and make damn sure you get a perfectly smooth surface before you get rolling. Little imperfections left when you start spraying will stand out like a whore in church once you get your shiny surface applied.

A couple things to keep in mind at this point are that you should try to do as much metal work as possible before you get moving with body filler. If you get carried away with it, it could break free after a few thousand miles under heavy throttle and there goes your shiny paint in a flash of high-speed disassembly on the interstate. Also, when using body filler, don't use too much or too little hardener, especially between coats because it makes for some really difficult sanding

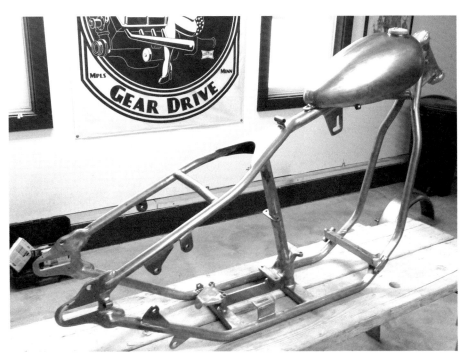

Here is how the sheet metal and frame looked when they showed up at the Painter's shop in Minnesota.

73

Jeremy has several specialty hangers for securing the parts for painting.

A base coat of primer is applied, this is the last chance to hide any blems.

Different paints will use different base coats, in our case it was black.

A great finish begins with hours of careful body work.

that could force you to start completely over.

Once you finish with your bodywork, it's time for some primer! The nice thing about primer/sealer is that you can start to see any little imperfections you may have missed when doing your bodywork. So now you have a chance to clean up what was overlooked before hand.

Finally, some color. In this case, Jeremy chose a black base-coat to start with here and this is step number one after all the bodywork and sealing.

Now is where it gets tricky. Here, Jeremy put on a healthy dose of gold metal-flake, and I can assure you that this is MUCH more difficult than it may seem. What needs to be done here involves laying down some clear and hosing on the metal-flake dry, right on top of the still wet clear. If you've ever had to spray paint around all 360 degrees of several pieces of tubing stuck together, you can understand the difficulty here, especially if you don't want it hanging off all of the low points.

So when blowing on the metal-flake, it may be necessary to do bits at a time. For instance, shoot one section with clear, then flake, and repeat further down the line. But you have to be quick because you don't want wet and dry lines overlapping each other and making for a rough surface.

After the base flake is all laid out and dried completely, you have to put on several coats of clear. See, the metal-flake will make the surface rough like you would imagine it would, so now is the time to smooth it all out, and several coats of clear will fill in around the flake and get you back to a new surface, but not before a bunch of wet sanding.

When spraying the sealer, paint, or clear, after several coats, the surface starts to turn into what people in the industry call an "orange peel" surface. In other words, it starts to get rough and bumpy like the rind of an orange. No, it's not just a clever name.

Now, remember when I said that these painters are multi-talented? Here is where the next facet comes into play. Not only do they have to have a fine tuned eye for perfection in making a smooth and even finish, but now is the time to integrate a complicated design into an already difficult project.

Jeremy took off with some one-eighth inch fine-line tape and laid out three different panels on the tank. This is the same design carved into the fender, but for simplicity's sake, we will only show the tank here because it has the most detail and the most steps to be laid out.

After the panels were masked off, Jeremy took a piece of lace and laid it out over the side panels for a nice background design. After the lace is stuck in place, a coat of red candy is sprayed over the top. Be careful here though, you don't want to get carried away. If you spray on too much or too little, you'll lose

Over the black Jeremy shot a heavy gold metal flake on everything.

The flake has to be buried on clear to keep it form sticking up and looking horrible.

A design like this is as much about the tape work as it is about the painting.

A translucent top coat will let varying amounts of the designs below come through the color.

With the tape completely removed here you can see exactly what I mean.

Today the addition of custom lettering has become very common.

too much of the lace pattern, and it will disappear later under more coats of candy.

After the red candy is laid down to reveal the lace pattern, Jeremy took some black base in his airbrush and put a nice fade around the entire outside of each panel. But let us not forget about the top panel. Here, Jeremy took and cut out a pattern of semi-circles in sequence, laid them out perpendicular to the direction of the bike, and sprayed just a small fade around the back-side of each circle. He then moved on ahead to the next row until finished. Another black fade around the entire outside of this panel, and we're ready to see what it looks like with another color!

Aside from just laying down a red candy over the top of it all, pay attention! Jeremy has not removed all of the masking here; the eight-inch fine line tape was left behind to keep a nice gold line to encompass each panel.

Nearby is the tank with the fine line tape removed. With little else to say about this pic, it would probably be a good place to mention that the fender came in for about the same process along with the frame, but the frame only got a red candy right after the base-flake and the clear. The only thing left for the frame at this point is the clear.

And yet another facet of this artist's many talents: lettering. Yes, Jeremy designed and cut these words of wisdom, as well as the double-thumbed fist and Mescaline button, from the late, great Doctor himself. The pattern is a sheet of vinyl sticker that will stick nicely to the tank and come off clean and easy as well. Now it's time to get into some goldleaf.

Goldleaf is not too bad if you have a delicate hand and some good patience. The stuff is WAY thin, and comes apart really easily, so be careful. Once the pattern is stuck where you want it, you take the correct glue for gold flake and evenly spread a thin coat of it on the exposed paint.

With the pattern removed and only the glue left, you take a thin piece of the foil and stick it to the tank. It goes without saying that the goldleaf will only stick to the glue, so after it's dry and the flake is stuck, you simply brush off the excess. Note the photo to see just how fragile the foil really is. Now you don't need to get too carried away with the brushing here, just take your time and be gentle.

After this comes many coats of clear with plenty of wet sanding to boot, but in between Jeremy shows off yet another talent, and this one is just as tricky, if not, more: the pinstriping around the gold flake. Now this is not a sticker or anything like that, Jeremy laid this on by hand, slowly and painstakingly. He is an excellent pinstriper at the worst.

After a good polish, we reveal the finished product. All of that time and effort into a single gas tank is well worth the effort. Not only is it an amazing piece of art by a very talented artist, but people get to ogle over it for years to come. If you take your time as you go through this lengthy process, you'll have a much better end result.

And now, after many sleepless nights and obscure sleeping accommodations, we push forward, headlong against the odds and beg for more. The paint fumes are heavy and the restless and sleep deprived nature of everybody involved is beginning to take its toll. We must push forward. We must finish. "The possibility of physical and mental collapse is now very real. No sympathy for the devil, keep that in mind. Buy the ticket. Take the ride..." -HST

At this point Jeremy went back and ran a thick outline to make the letters stand out even more. Then, after multiple coats of clear with sanding between, the whole thing comes together.

This lettering can be as simple as being painted on, or as detailed as using gold or silver-leaf.

This goldleaf is a very delicate material and takes a gentle hand.

12
SADDLE WORK

SOLO SEAT & PAD

RAW SEAT PAN

MATCHING FRONT/REAR SOLO

HAND TOOLED LEATHER SEAT

CUSTOM LEATHER ON STEEL PAN

KING/QUEEN

What is a high-speed death machine without an uncomfortable place to plant your hairy ass? Blasting across the country at half the speed of sound doesn't require a fancy seat, but in the case that you want to have some aesthetically pleasing leather to adorn your scooter and you don't feel that tassels hanging off your hand controls is the way to accomplish this, I'll try to walk you through the appropriate steps to carve a design into some rawhide. Now, we weren't all born with the talent of Christian Marsh at Xian Leather, but if you want flawless perfection, go to him. He is the paradigm of leather tooling and I've been ruining my health trying to figure out how he makes it look so good.

But before you dive in head long, you're going to need the proper equipment, and there is quite the variety of tools out there to meet your needs. I'm only going to cover the very basics here so that you don't wind up putting thousands of dollars into something you may never do again. Also, I'll explain the necessary tools as we move along so that you can see just exactly what I'm talking about. The seat I built for this book was a commission from a friend of mine, Kim Hofer, and it fit the bill here.

Now I've never read a book on leather tooling, and just kind of heard some theory from the Asian fellow that owns the local store where I get my equipment, so this may deviate from the normal practice. After probably a couple hundred different projects under my belt, I've developed my own technique, and it works really well for me, and here it is. Now let's get hammering. First thing's first: Get your pan mounted to your death trap where you're good and comfortable. When you've finished, send it off to chrome. If you want, you can leave some exposed, like this seat for instance, or get some paint on it so the exposed under-side won't rust. You can also just let it rust if that's your bag. From here out, decide what you want where and cut yourself a pattern. (Note: Usually I drill holes after the leather is stuck in place, but this was a re-do.)

Now you'll take and draw out what you want on your livestock skin. I usually lay it out rough, then work out the details, but make sure you fully draw it all out so that you're certain that you'll like it. Now it's time to get yourself some leather.

There are a few things you should know about leather selection. I usually use four or five ounce tooling leather because it's heavy enough to hold up under severe conditions but it's light enough to work with when shaping. Be sure that it's "tooling" leather though, and if you can, look it over so that you don't get a piece with cuts, brands or thin spots in it.

Next, you'll take your pattern and lay it out on your leather. From here, it's as simple as cutting out your soon-to-be, beautiful ass perch. This would be the perfect place to say that you should be sure that your hands stay clean while you're tooling, because that leather will soak up any contaminates on your hands, and there is NO getting it out. Don't overhaul your greasy four-speed right before you jump on your leatherwork.

To get your design into the leather, you can just skip right to cutting – if you're confident enough - but I like to give myself an idea first. Your first step is to wet the TOP side of the leather. I was told to use a moist sponge, but you wind up with too much moisture this way. I decided to try a spray bottle and it turned out to be much easier to control how wet you want it and precisely

A good custom leather seat can really set your bike apart from the crowd, a great one is even better.

Here is a metal seat pan ready for a custom leather covering.

If you are not able to draw yourself, a brother with a tattoo parlor can hook you up.

You can buy sections of leather like this at any Tandy Leather shop.

Wetting down the leather will help in the transfer of the design.

Giving yourself a good layout will help give you a good guide for the rest of the tooling.

where. For the layout, just give the top side a good squirt. You'll probably have to go over it two or three times before it stops soaking up all the water but you want to get it to where the surface stays wet after a minute.

Now, in the spirit of saving you some money on unnecessary tools, to get your art laid out on the cow flesh, use a Bic mechanical pencil with no lead. Use just the side, which will require you to hold it at a bit of an angle. Straight up will get too wide. Then, you lay it out. One thing to note here is that once you do this, there is no getting it out, so go lightly and be precise.

These are the very basic tools you'll need: a swivel knife with a twenty-some-thing degree blade, (don't use the ceramic blades, they aren't sharp enough) a few punches, (a medium and a narrow beveller, maybe a medium and a pointed back-grounder, or a pear stamp or two) and a hammer. You can get much better hammers, but I like the cheap wooden hammers because they are lighter, so you can do some very intricate hammering with them.

Now you simply cut over your pattern you scratched in the leather. Be sure to hold your knife straight up and down so that you don't undercut. This will make for some unfriendly changes in your art when you get into hammering. Also, be sure to keep your knife good and sharp. I sharpen between every seat. The stropping that people suggest has never done me any good; it's up to you though. And last, it is unnecessary to push extra hard here. That knife will only go so deep anyway, so be rather gentle and keep it moving, it makes for much better lines this way.

Here is where I'm sure I differ from about everybody else. I stain my design at this point rather than after hammering, and here is why. When you get into hammering, for some reason, the stain makes for MUCH more smooth hammering. The exception is if you are doing some backgrounding with a stippled punch of some sort, do that first. Since there was none on this seat, I dove right in to staining.

I just use a series of brushes to apply the stain, and obviously you need some fine brushes for the tight spots. Staining is rather difficult because there is absolutely NO room for error here, since it will not come out. Also note that the moisture content will severely affect how the leather soaks up the stain. If it's really wet, it's easier to stain because the leather doesn't soak it up nearly as easy, but it looks worse when it dries and you're done. So, if you're putting it on dry, don't get too much stain on the leather, especially in the tight places near the boarders because the piece you don't want stained could soak up stain as well. Then your seat will go flying across the room near the trash can in a furious rage of irrational anger. I've seen it a thousand times!

Staining can be tough, so make sure to practice plenty before you start to lay it out on the seat that you've invested so much time and money into. And play around with it. You may find that you can manipulate the stain in odd ways to work in your favor. Note also that when selecting stain, you should search for the most volatile shit you can find. Anything good for the environment is not good for leatherwork.

Now I hammer. See, most people, I understand, usually do this before the stain and I would suggest trying it just to see the differences. Plus it's more difficult to see how you're doing on top of stain, but I have always liked the end result much more. When beveling, I find it best to tilt the punch in just a bit so you're barely hammering out towards the bevel. Then, go over it again, hammering much lighter, with the punch straight up and down. It seems to take out the individual hammer marks and smooth it all out. Also, when hammering, imagine your picture in three dimensions so as to know

Here is a look at the basic tools you will need to get started in this craft. These are also available from Tandy.

One last step before tooling is to cut over all the lines from your transfer.

You can purchase a complete line of paints and dyes from any leather shop for your projects. Fiebings are made right in Wisconsin.

Hand painting stain on the leather can give you greater control of the look of the design.

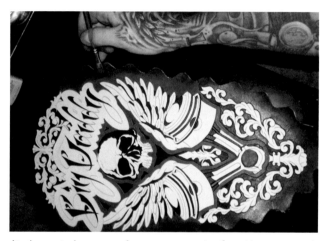

It does take a serious amount of patience and technique so practice, practice, practice.

There are about a million tools for hammering leather into a three dimensional design and each one achieves a different effect.

where to bevel and get the correct depth out of it.

Concerning hammering, I differ as well. I was told to keep the leather rather wet when hammering, but I've come to find that you can get much deeper bevels and backgrounds if you let it dry out a bit. I usually wet the backside really well, until it starts to bleed through the topside just a bit here and there. Then just mist on a very light layer on top, and let it dry for about five to ten minutes. When you start to see a lighter color on the surface, it's just about right. Then, as it starts to really dry out, just hit the topside with a moderate misting. The theory here is to keep the center wet, and the outside dry. The beveling sticks tight this way. I found if you hammer while it's too wet, your hammering comes out a bit and you lose dimension.

Here you also want to finish up any staining that may have magically appeared after hammering and also get the edges. I didn't have room for another picture, so I'll just say here that if you're leaving exposed edges, you'll want to round them with a leather edging tool and some saddle soap to make it all nice and clean and round and fancy. But save this for the end; you can't stain through the soap.

You can go many different ways with color selection. You could leave the raw leather exposed if you wanted, and that is where I mention that leather changes its appearance with time. See how the raw leather looks almost white? Well, inside of a month in the sun, the leather will turn darker and your tooling will stand out much more. Also, stain and antiquing gels will change colors as well. If the stain appears to be far too dark or blotchy when you first apply it, it will lighten up and even out as it dries.

Now for the antiquing gel; this stuff is great. It really makes your tooling stand out, and it's rather easy to work with, unless you want it light. Then it's tough because you have to work quickly to fill in all the crevices and wipe it all of in one fell swoop. This stuff also responds to the leather's moisture content as well and you can manipulate it in your favor. For instance, if it's dry, you can lay it on quickly and heavily, then wipe the high spots off with a semi-wet sponge to make it lighter. And you can skip this step all together if you want, or use it as the only color in place of any stain.

Like I said earlier, this customer wanted it dark, so I laid it on heavy and let it dry a bit before I wiped it off. Just keep in mind that this stuff is water soluble, so you can go over and over it, even if it gets sticky or wads up while you're wiping it.

Another option, if you want to make it even darker, is to use a lighter colored antique or stain, then wipe on black really lightly on the high spots. But be careful here, you'll want to use very high thread count material and soak only a small portion of your cloth with stain, then wipe damn near all of it off on a towel or something that will soak up most of the stain from your cloth. You want to have to really work hard to get even the slightest amount of color from it. It will seem like you're polishing the leather and it's slowly getting darker. Again, keep very little on the rag.

Now, using a darker stain on the high spots to finish and a lighter antique underneath, will make your beveling and backgrounding much lighter than the high spots, and can make for a nice look, if you do it right. It usually works best to go from dark around the edges to light, or even non-existent in the middle. The last step is to apply some finish of some sort, and also keep in mind that the finish will take off some of your antiquing gel, or stain on the high spots, so going just a touch overboard on the color is nothing to worry about entirely.

Here is the finished product, and for a space restriction, I won't fill a whole other chapter on how to mount it, but it's rather

Here you can really see the different uses of color on this seat.

This would be the end of this project if we were going to let it age naturally from the sun.

Instead Lemme is going to give it an aged look by antiquing it with a gel.

In this picture you can really see how colorful the end design is. Against the chrome seat pan it will be incredible.

From here the finished custom seat can be mounted with or without any additional padding.

This one will simply get attached to the seat pan by gluing it down, drilling and riveting it to the pan.

The heavier you apply this chemical and the longer you leave it on before wiping will determine how dark comes out.

straightforward. Padding is optional, and I usually put it on, unless requested otherwise, because it makes for a nice look. Just make the padding smaller than the leather by about an inch around the edges, and glue it on the pan. Then glue your fresh new leather on and rivet the thing down.

It makes life much easier to wet the leather to form it around the padding, but be careful or you could wind up smudging the finish on the topside while it's wet. It's a fickle hellcat, but just use some finesse and wet the backside only. Let it dry out entirely after it's fit, then glue it down to make its shape hold. Then drill holes (VERY CAREFULLY) and rivet. Presto! You've got yourself a fine piece of equipment to share with your ass!

The Importance of Pappy's Shack

As I was growing up in stump-pull Pennsylvania, there were many people influential in my development as a journeyman philosopher: biker. Most of these people I met one after another while trying to learn how to keep my old Shovelhead on the road. The place where all this activity was fostered was a little 20 x 20 garage built out of leftover lumber with a concrete floor, poured three or four feet at a time. It sat at the top of a hill

I'm sure it used to be the site of championship hill climbs and was the family garage of my brother Scotty. We all called it Pappy's shack.

We were all poor as hell back then and once you had the money to buy a bike, more than likely a used one, you needed the support of everyone around you to keep it on the road without spending the rent money every month to do it. I learned a lot of things in that little place, helped on many projects and even built a few of my own bikes. When it came to learning a new skill, we just went at it. Maybe we weren't right all the time, but we were doing it and that's where it's at! Everything from paint to frame raking, collision repair to engine rebuilds, it all happened in the shack. If you were ever in the middle of making your bike pretty when a workin' stiff rolled up with a cracked frame or broken starter, then you got pushed outside and pitched in to help get this "point A to B machine" ready for the work week.

It's almost hard for me to believe that not that long ago, places like Pappy's shack were not only an important part of the culture, but were essential to the basic survival of motorcycling itself. The men in this sport, and maybe the time I'm waxing nostalgic of, had more concerns about keeping food on the table and gas in the car than how many inches a motor had, or whose forward controls were on a bike. It was a great time to be alive and made me grateful for the good things we have today.

Pappy's Shack – Chris's First Shared Space

13

WIRING SIMPLIFIED

WIRE ENDS

HEAT SHRINK

ON OFF

COIL

HEAD LAMP

SOLDERING IRON (HOT)

SOLDER

VOLTAGE REGULATOR

STATOR

#1

CIRCUIT BREAKER

WIRE .10 GA. .12 GA. .18 GA.

GROUND

#2

CIRCUIT BREAKER

Wiring can be the hardest part of building your own custom bike, or the easiest if you have the right frame of mind going into it. Today's aftermarket offers a wide variety of harness kits and all-in-one switch housing solutions to make it easier. Simplified wiring, or chopper wiring, just doesn't have to be complicated. Master this and it becomes easier to add on to that basic system if you want to include extra lights, turn signals, etc. The best advice here can be in the preparation you build into your wiring to begin with. You have to imagine the weather and torture, vibration, heat, all these factors may cause parts of your harness to fail. By realizing that in advance and building your wiring correctly, you will have little trouble on the road.

We mentioned in the beginning of this book that magazine articles can be a good resource for things like this. But when it comes to tech articles on simple wiring, some fall short. See, most tech articles you'll read seem to be much alike and rather mundane. Usually, the person explaining the process has a firm grasp on the situation and has done it a zillion times but lacks the words to convey the idea which is fine unless you have no idea what they are talking about. So, what winds up happening is something like Stephen Hawking attempting to explain Quantum Mechanics to some kid flippin' burgers at McDonalds. We thought for the purpose of this book we might try to do a little less step-by-step and try to explain some theory here in a (poor) attempt to get the reader to bend their mind around the reasons for assembling this crazy electrical shit in a certain fashion. That being said, here we go!

First thing's first, we are not wiring up a set of speakers for the living room here, it is rather a solid-mounted, high-horsepower death machine that is constantly trying to vibrate itself completely apart. So, we must make it solid or you will be left on the side of the road in the middle of the desert, dying of dehydration and trying to avoid the ensuing vultures who want little more then to disembowel you.

A good selection of wiring tools and accessories is an important part of any tool catalogue.

For this reason, we must tell you that the simple twisting of wires, basic crimping or any other juvenile method of attaching wires should be thrown out. As for the little plastic shrouds on your wire ends, pull them off and throw them over your shoulder, eat them, whatever, just make sure you never see them again.

Don't even think about using those horrible plastic collars; ditch them.

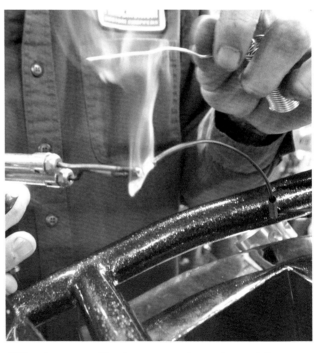

Whether you like it or not, there is nothing better than a soldered connection. A little ventilation is a good thing here.

Now, after the wire is stripped, you crimp the end on and solder that connection so well that it will never come apart.

Throw some heat shrink over the newly soldered connection to keep out the elements and you'll have yourself a good, solid piece of equipment to work with. It should be said at this point that when connecting two wires and/or splicing, the same soldering process should be followed.

Now for a quick run through what goes where and why. (Refer to my hand drawn schematic to make less sense on the matter.) For the electronically deficient, or anyone lacking the education or any knowledge of electricity whatsoever, the thought here is to start at the battery with the largest wire on the bike and work your way gradually towards smaller size wires as you get towards the ends.

See, when you start at the battery, your ground wire needs to be much larger than the others, as does the initial positive wire because you are feeding several different instruments off of that one single wire.

It looks a little crazy but a wiring harness for a chopper can be as simple as this.

So, it needs to be a beefy sum bitch to handle all of this electrical insanity or else it will break the circuit via the circuit breaker working properly and doing its job, or catch fire and burn your whole damn bike to the ground on the side of the road in an inferno of inadequate wiring. One or the other...

Moving on, depending on your situation, you could run many wires to many parts and it would be just fine. However, if you need shit hidden for aesthetic purposes, well, then, this is a horse of a different color. In theory, you could run one wire through one breaker and one switch, but your chances of disaster, like breaking the breaker, are ramped up a bit. Now keep in mind that you can combat this sometimes inevitable situation by installing a second breaker right beside the primary one, but not wiring it in. This way when your primary breaker goes when you're out in the middle of some out-back, hill-folk infested area you can simply switch your wires over to the secondary and be on your way rather than winding up like Jon Voigt and Burt Reynolds in Deliverance.

Before I get further into the "how," I want to explain some more "why." Looking back at my diagram, you can sure as shit run two wires from the battery, individually, to each breaker. I wired them

A motorcycle gets pounded by the elements so heat shrink should also be part of any connection.

Starting with good solid battery cables will make your project trouble free down the road.

Circuit breakers can not be omitted as far as I am concerned. I've seen a bike burst into flames or just sit and smoke from a lack of breakers.

Keeping wires hidden and away from moving parts will give you a clean look and fewer hassles down the road.

The headlight is a great place to hide wiring on a chopper. We put a three position toggle switch inside the '49 headlight shell.

one-off-the-other just for simplicity's sake. Also, you can not run the voltage regulator to the initial breaker. If you connect the regulator to the wiring harness directly, you will not be able to shut your bike off with the switch. When you go to shut it off, it will just keep running all the way into infinity and you will look like an asshole in front of a crowd of people. It's not fun.

Now, the circuit is run in a loop from positive to negative and then through the battery the other way in a constant circle of electronic marathon. So, to get the power to say, your headlight, you'll have power in and also some sort of ground going back to the negative side of the battery, in order to again complete this endless cycle of electronic madness. In between, you have a series of breakers -in case things go haywire- and switches for turning things on and off. Add a brake switch here or there and it is as simple as that! In the case of the '49 Pan here, the ground is on the body of the headlight and the toggle switch is contained within to select high or low beam.

The ignition works the same way. Power goes in one end of the coil, and out the other. Actually, there are two bundles of wire inside the coil, juice runs through the primary winding and through the (closed) points to ground – creating a magnetic field. When the points open the juice running through the primary winding is interrupted and the field collapses – over the secondary winding. This creates one hell of a spark just a little before the piston hits TDC.

A good manual will take you through any other more than basic wiring needs but before we let you out of this chapter, how about a few more tips like the use of Dielectric grease? For anyone who is determined to ride their bike you will surely come across your fair share of less than good weather. This is why we apply a liberal amount of Dielectric grease at every electrical connection. This includes: plugs, headlights, taillights, anyplace that water can get in and cause corrosion; Dielectric grease will keep it out.

A nice light gauge steel wire is a good thing to have in the case of running wires through your frame to keep them out of sight. It's easier to slide a section of steel wire into a frame and fish it around than it is to do it with a piece of electrical wire. Just a small bend on the end and you can pull the wire through from one hole to the other.

Expect the unexpected. As we mentioned in the beginning, there is nothing that sucks like a broken or shorted wire on the side of the road. Take time to look at all your connections and think about what you might be able to do to make them more secure or able to fend off the elements better. In the case shown here, we decided to add some small sections of rubber hose held on by black ATV to protect the tops of our circuit breakers.

This is another place on the build that we must warn against being in a hurry. A little extra time spent here can save you hours and hours down the road, or worse yet, on the side of the road. Trust the years of experience behind this book from cats who have traveled that path and been stuck somewhere waiting for the parts' store to open in the morning; you're almost done, slow down.

Wiring can be a great way to customize too. Cloth type wires, even plug wires, have a great look.

Planning for the elements is job one. The use of dielectric grease will keep the water out.

A small gauge steel "pull wire" will help when running wires through the frame.

Here is our hidden circuit breaker solution for the '49 project.

14

ROADSIDE'S SWAP MEET BUILD

Okay, so Wildman and I were talkin' about how we both sort of started into this whole thing with stock modification. At that time, we didn't have a fancy term for it, it was just what we had to do to have a bike and trick it out. We thought that a swap meet rehab would be the perfect fit for a beginners' guide to custom bike building so we laid out the plan that went into my bike: Chick Magnet.

Today, the scene has gone in and out of the money phase but for a lot of us, the benefits of stock mod are just as essential as they always have been. Regardless of what they tell you on television, it does not take $160,000 to have a cool-ass custom bike and as an example, the sum total of what went into the Chick Magnet was a measly $4,000. This should be proof that anyone with a nominal amount of mechanical skill, and the ability

to ask for help, can have a "Low Budget Rocker."

To get things started, we traveled up north to, where through the help of Fab Kevin, I took an old '79 FL swingarm frame through the process of installing a weld-on hardtail. So, here's the deal; I got the frame from a long time friend, Steve Marabella. Steve runs a little thing on the side called "Blue Collar Choppers," and he was looking for a tank he needed. I traded him a wrecked Evo style Sporty fuel tank for the frame and since the tank was something another cat gave to me, I didn't technically have any money in it. However, if you don't have the inventory to work this kind of a deal, you could expect to find a frame like this at most swap meets for around $150: not a bad investment.

Roadside bends tubes with a manual bender for the frame rails which will build the hardtail section of the FL, using 1 ¼ inch tubing.

New stock style rear axle forgings shown here can be purchased for $300-$350. These will be used to construct the new rear section.

Blue tape shows the general areas where cuts will be made, to remove the old rear section of the frame.

Next, the lower frame rails are heated by hand and bent using an alignment tool that Fab Kevin made by hand.

Roadside holds the frame section while Fab Kevin slices and dices. The portable band saw makes short work of this step. Kevin even let Roadside cut, until he broke the blade.

Two cuts are made along the side of the seat post tube and both upper frame rails are heated and bent to be parallel with the backbone.

Here, the axle forgings are placed into the frame jig and after alignment is checked, they are ready to receive slugs.

Here, you can see how the slugs are used to bring the new frame rails into the existing frame.

Now, the whole frame is put into the jig and checked for alignment and to make sure everything is straight. The line helps as a reference.

With the slugs and frame rails tapped together, frame is checked for alignment once more. From the back, you can see the steering neck, frame rails and axle plates are 100% in line.

Dan Roedel, Kevin's motor guy, lends a hand at this point in the creation of the slugs. In a lathe, he trims some of the thickness from the slugs so they'll fit into the forgings.

Can you see how clean and organized Kevin's shop is? It further goes to prove what we've said about organization.

Kevin tack welds the rails, a few tacks at a time so that the heat doesn't distort the metal and put the axle plates out of position, then inspects the welds for penetration, after they're in place and cool, he finishes them up.

In this step, Roadside fish mounts a frame rail that will be used as his top frame support, and also mounts the seat springs and oil bag. After he has a good fit, this gets welded in.

In the final pic, you can see the upper frame rails are parallel with backbone; the frame looks perfectly straight. Roadside used a Muskrat seat kit and Lucky Charms' oil bag.

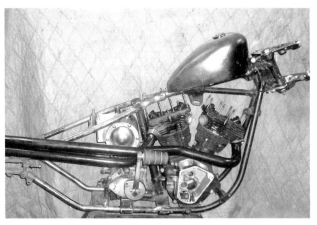

With the frame fresh back from Fab Kevin's, we begin the mock-up just to get a look at how things are going to go. This also gives me the opportunity to set up the pipes.

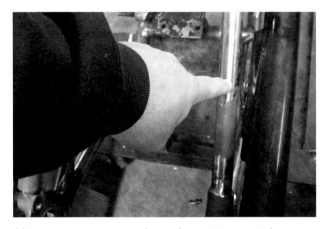

Here you can see where I want to put the mounting brackets for the pipes on the frame.

The Shovel I paid a grand for had an oil pump failure and we had take it apart. It ended up being a partial rebuild.

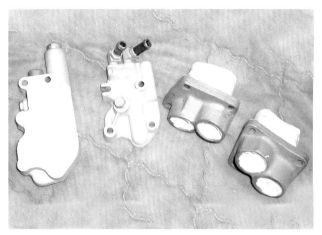

The original oil pump and lifter blocks were usable, but I wanted some bling so I replaced these with new Sifton parts.

I got this set of 2002 FXDWG lowers for $20 and the forward controls for $125. I ended up trading the legs for narrow glide legs.

I paid $20 for this S&S Super E carb. Note the white spot in the breather hole. It needed a rebuild, but with a $30 kit, a new carbon block and some elbow grease, it's like new.

Here's a 21 inch front wheel that cost me $50, and it even came with the tire. The rear cost me the same; it's from a 2003 Heritage Softail, but didn't come with a tire.

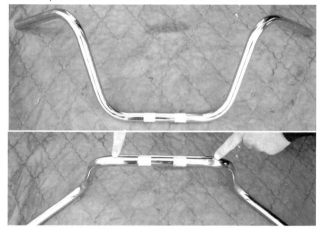

I got these bars for free but they had wiring holes in them. My buddy Kramer welded the holes and once powdercoated, no one knew the difference.

These tabs can be picked up, premade, at any hot rod shop. They're a great fit for our pipe mounts. Tommy (Hot Rods by Tommy) welded them in place for our pipes.

Notice how clean these look once they're in place and the pipes are mounted.

Here's the brake anchor tab that Fab Kevin graciously supplied with his rear caliper set-up. We welded it into place and it was perfect.

Using the time honored tradition of 3/8 hose taped to the rear wheel, we provide the spacing to mount our rear fender.

We set the fender in place and decide what location looks best. Eleven o'clock it is, and some indication marks are made to locate the mounts.

Here you can see Tommy's brilliant plan come to life. The fender is returned to our desired position and the mounts are in place for welding: a perfect fit.

As you can see here, we have drilled pilot holes in both struts and are now using a chamfer bit to dress up the outside edge of our finished holes: never too many details.

Measuring two pieces of quarter inch stainless steel flat stock, we lay out what will be our fender struts.

Rather than using a nut on the back side of my axle forging, Tommy suggested tapping them out since they had so much meat. This gives us a threaded fit of the fender struts.

After a little bending, the struts are in place. You can see how good the Harley forging mounts worked out, keeping it nice and clean.

Here's a close-up of the strut mounting. Also in this shot is the beautiful five-dollar Harley rotor I scored. I got the front one for another five.

At the top of the struts, we tapped out the struts themselves to accept two smaller bolts that mount the fender to them on each side.

I welded a piece of square stock to the neck, again with the help of Tommy, and built the stops back up with a spare piece of aluminum and a welder.

Here she is, all ready for disassembly and paint work. All the sheet metal was boxed up and sent out to Darren at Liquid Illusions.

These are some 39mm trees I picked up for $20, from Kyle at Pensacola H-D. You can see here that the stops have been knocked off. E

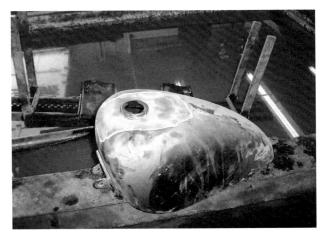

It's always a good idea to have a radiator shop seal your tank. In addition to pressure testing and welding, their red coat sealer is the best.

After the tank comes back, Darren tapes up the filler bung and petcock, then sandblasts any flash rust and impurities in the metal.

When the primer is dry the next morning, he sprays a guide coat of rattle can black to make sure all sand scratches and low spots are eliminated during the final sanding.

Darren applies a thin skim coat of bondo and then starts the sanding with some 36 grit and a sanding block, before moving on to finer grits.

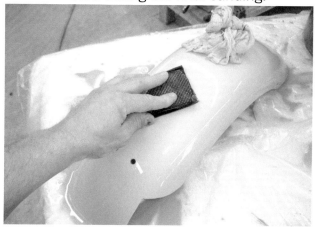

Using a piece of 400 grit wet/dry sandpaper, Darren sands the tank and rear fender.

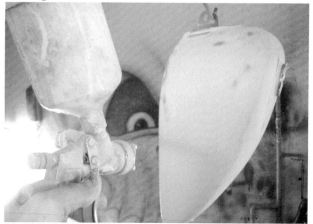

Darren mixes up some PPG global primer. He applies 3 to 4 heavy coats, allowing ten to fifteen minutes of flash time between each one.

After 3 to 4 coats of House of Kolor black base coat, he grabs a roll of blue fine line and tapes out a set of traditional flames.

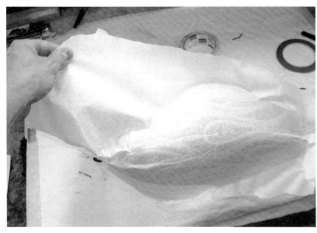

Then the entire tank is covered with masking paper and smoothed out. You can get a roll of this transfer paper at your local sign shop.

Once the yellow has dried, he uses the air-brush and adds some orange, red and violet highlights to the flames.

With a new razor blade, he traces the blue line tape, only cutting through the masking paper not the tape.

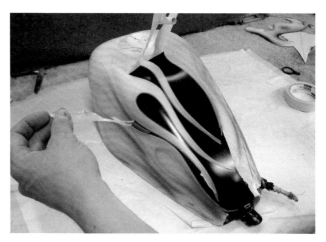

When all the airbrush work is done, it's time to remove all the masking and tape. Next, the pieces get 3 coats of PPG global clear.

After removing the tape from inside the flames, he starts by spraying 3 coats of white, followed by 3 coats of House of Kolor yellow pearl base coat.

After the clear has dried and the tank is wet sanded, it's ready for some blue pinstripes.

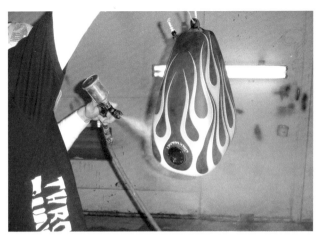

Once the pinstripes have dried and the tagline "Chick Magnet" is added under the filler neck, the tins are ready for the final clear.

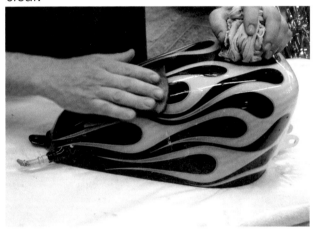

Yes, more wet sanding to knock down the bumps.

When the raised edges from the pinstripes are sanded smooth, the tins are buffed out to a shiny gloss using a wool buffing pad and some 3M compound.

So here we are, about 40 hours and around $4,000 invested, three swap meets, a couple of trades and the bike is back together. Of course none of this could be achieved without the help of my friends; thank you all. I almost can't wait to get the next project started. Until then, go find some cool shit to bolt together, we did!

15

CHRIS' MODIFIED AFTERMARKET BUILD

So this bike was for me, a lifetime in the making. You see, back in the late seventies I was a young man building plastic Revell model choppers. They were long crazy rails with skulls and I wanted one so bad I could taste it. Well, some thirty-plus years later, I have never been able to get those bikes out of my head. It wouldn't be settled until I just built one of the damn things and got it over with. It all came to a head when my boy Tim from Papa Clutch traded me on this '49 Panhead motor.

What I set out to do in this was build a traditional seventies hippy freak machine, sticking to old traditions but blending in some new technology. To do this, I enlisted the help and guidance of Paughco, who I knew could deliver the goods, and their man Jason who would steer me through the right and wrong choices to achieve the bike of my dreams. Instead of making everything from scratch, I would do it, as they did in the seventies, with what I could get from the aftermarket and some used parts that could be modified to be more personal and a little more custom. Other than a few modifications on the frame geometry, the bike you see here is exactly what I had in mind all the time.

Of course, once the UPS guy drops off the boxes, the whole thing has to start with a quick mock-up and a night of standing around talking about how bad-ass it's going to be.

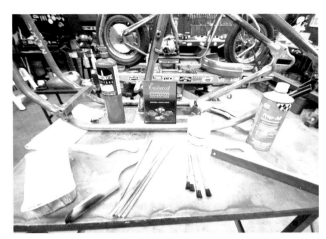

The Eastwood Company would provide a kit for lead soldering that came with a handy DVD . . .

In its delivered state, the Paughco frame was solid and a good deal, but needed a lot of time to achieve that clean, molded, custom look.

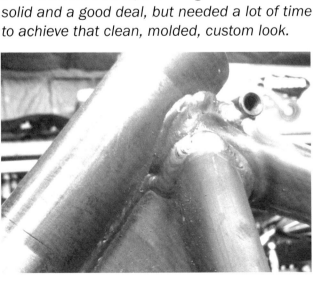

Here you can see areas that we molded using a method my old man did back in the body shop days, lead soldering.

. . .and before long we were applying the tinning butter. . .

. . .putting in the lead and paddling it out smooth.

Here you can see me working the hot lead.

The finish came out great, after a few lessons in what not to do, the end result is that the rust will not come through like putty.

We also decided to shape the rear wheel flanges a little bit as well. Nothing too radical, we just knocked off the square edges.

Working Lead

Lead is old-skool and durable, but also toxic:

1. Provide ventilation to avoid inhaling fumes.
2. Wear gloves and wash hands prior to eating or smoking.
3. Wear goggles and a mask for grinding.
4. Vacuum up the dust instead of sweeping.

Ed.

There was still a ton of work to be done with 2 inch Rol-Loc sanding discs and tapers. My brother Rob's son, Robbie, put in the overtime helping me get it done in time.

One item I almost overlooked was the underside of the frame at the down tube. I thought about looking into those Pan lids and seeing this.

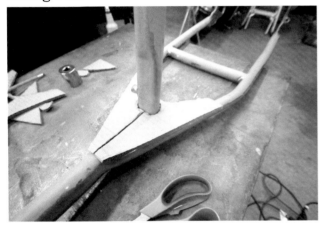

I cut out a quick little template that I sent over to my machine shop guys to cut out of steel plate.

Using some clamps, I held the edge tight and tacked it into place.

When it came back, I tacked it to the down tube and heated one side at a time and hammered it into place against the frame rail.

After trimming away some of the extra metal from the edge, I fired up the Lincoln TIG and locked it down.

The finished plate was a great move and I knew once we mocked the motor up and I looked into the reflection of those Pans, it would be all I could see.

One of the finishing touches was a pair of Fab Kevin's axle sliders. It's a pretty easy installation: drill the holes, thread them and you're done.

Next, we sprayed down a layer of basic primer to get a look at where we were with our frame molding. This lets you see the areas that need more work.

At this point, we do what we should have done in step one, and borrow a motor to double check our mounting-hole alignment.

Before going any further, we also installed our neck cups in the frame. The top cup was pretty easy.

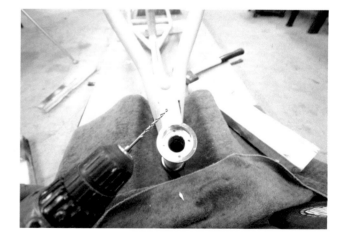

The bottom cup had internal fork stops so it took a little more work: four holes at a quarter inch depth.

Four dowel pins then tapped into place with a drift. You can see the tab here that will stop the frontend.

So we decided to take a little break and perform another mock-up to see what we were looking at. Some blue, low adhesive tape is a good idea for shiny stuff now.

It's the same thing on the bottom tree of the frontend. This time the holes are in place so just installing the pins was all that was required.

It was around this time that we got another shipment of boxes from Paughco.

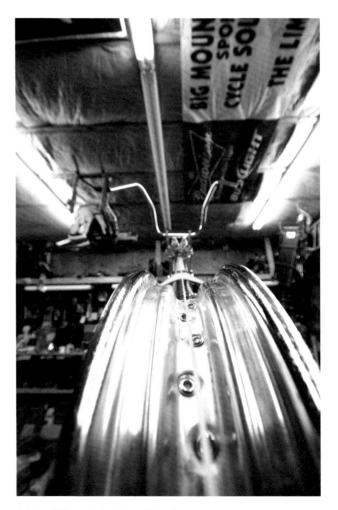

Using the string method, we center our rear wheel and measure for spacers.

I had an old GMA stand up brake caliper that I wanted to use so I headed over to Fish Machine. They also made necessary spacers.

With a little bit of extra time, I decided to work on the front wheel. I wanted to swap out the stock hub with a JR Cycle's spool hub.

The machined part looks killer with the Indian Larry brake rotor. With the spacers sorted out, we tear everything back off for a final sanding.

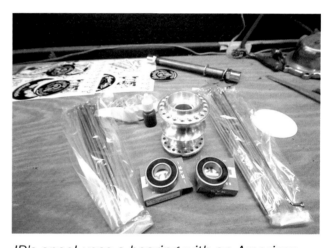

JR's spool uses a bearing with an American I.D. and a metric O.D. Once Buchanan's Stainless Spokes came in, we tore the old wheel down.

Next, I turn Robbie loose and he gets the frame to near-perfect condition.

Using our arbor press, we pressed the bearings in. Remember to install the spacer between them or do it twice like I did.

Rob Keller had experience with dirt bike wheel lacing so he came in to help out. Due to the design of this hub, all the spokes had to be in the hub before it could go into the wheel.

After we figured out the pattern (thanks to help from Buchanan's) it was on to the truing stand for a few hours of tweaking.

After we get it in shape, we take it to Bakerstown Radiator to get it pressure tested and cleaned with acid.

Our Paughco peanut tank needs a little dressing up. A flapper disc and some tappers will do the job but go slow, you don't want any leaks.

A day later it gets a dose of redcoat sealer. This makes a membrane on the inside of the tank that seals it ten times better than cream.

Back on the bike we're still not happy with where the tank mounts in its stock position. Through some convincing, I cut the front mount off and go to it.

We start off by using transfer punches to locate the center of our mount locations and then drill the hole to accept threaded bungs.

Once they were welded in and finished, the other guys were right, this was way better.

Now with the tank installed, you can see how much better it sits on the frame rail; nice and even and easy to take on and off. Remember the anti-seize!

Next was a set of six bends from Paughco that I loved. Only problem was, and this was my fault, the width didn't allow them to mount flush.

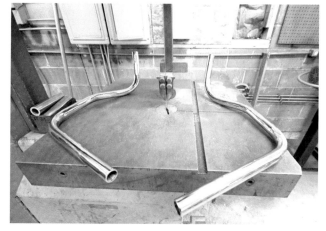

I couldn't believe I was cutting my brand new handlebars in half, but to use the parts I wanted, they would need an inch and a half added to the width.

I machined down a two-piece insert from similar wall tubing to gain the extra width.

Here is our flat strap style fender from Paughco in its delivered condition. The radius is all wrong for our build and we will need to address this.

I clamped them to the table and measured everything to be sure it was all square before welding it solid.

Using a couple pieces of motorcycle chain, we establish space for the fender to sit off of the wheel. We then take the fender to a manual shrinker.

After we spent some time with the flapper wheel and DA sander, slowly bringing down the welds and feathering out the metal, the seams almost disappear.

Here you can see it in use. As the jaws of the stretcher are pressed down, it forces the metal together and changes the radius.

Paul helped me out here by running the fender on the English wheel to flatten the top back out. From there I spent time with a hammer and a dolly to smooth out the sides.

Now the fender fit but needed personality. I took a piece of 1/4 inch round stock and welded it around the edge with silica bronze filler rod because it takes less heat on the TIG.

After some sanding, we place the whole thing on the tire and it fits like a glove. The look was a damn sight better as well and a piece right out of chopper history.

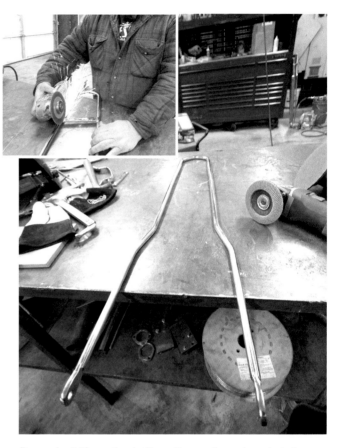

By using the stock Paughco sissy bar I got one that was symmetrical that I could jazz up without frustration. After I took the stock mounts off, I slowly brought the excess welds and mounts down. Remember, start with the flapper disc, go out further with the DA and feather the work area out.

Finally, we start on the serious mock-up. With a borrowed Pan motor from Cycle Warehouse in Butler, PA, we start to install the driveline.

After we bolt down the motor and tranny, loosely, we install the inch and a half BDL primary belt drive and run a straight edge from the front pulley to the rear. Adjust the tranny and motor to get everything square and lock them down.

Running the straight edge from the tranny sprocket to the rear wheel indicates the need for a sprocket spacer to ensure proper alignment. In our case it was 400 thousandths.

With the driveline in place, we can make our mounts for the fender and weld them in place. Two on the sissybar, two at the crossbar of the frame and one at the bottom of the fender.

With the fender in place, we can start to add the doodads. We made some mounts for the mufflers and Lemme helped me weld them on. These need to be strong structural welds so it was best to ask a pro!

I picked the spot and made additional mounts for the rear foot pegs and we welded them on as well.

With our Paughco Cocktail Shakers in place, we could start making our exhaust.

I wanted a particular look from these pipes so we used Paughco's builder kit and started from the back moving forward.

The kit comes with a selection of bends, straight pieces and two head pipes that you can use to make it happen. Go slow and cut a little each time.

In one of our final steps to this point, Lemme welds on a Fab Kevin seat-hinge mount. We had to wait for the fender to be mounted to make sure the seat sat in exactly the right spot.

From here we tore it down to send it out for paint. It was amazing that it only took like 15 minutes - after the weeks of getting it to this point.

With the frame and sheet metal back from the painter we begin final assembly. To start with, each and every mounting hole must be cleaned and tapped out.

Daniel preps the surface of the engine mounts by cleaning the paint away.

Next, we get the rear wheel and brake components installed.

Here's an old trick I am surprised more of the young guys don't know today for dealing with a freshly painted frame. Prop the motor up on blocks – sideways...

Now, it's the tranny plate and transmission.

... then slide the frame over the engine. Simple math; the frame is lighter and easier to maneuver than the engine.

After we pack the bearings, we install the Paughco Springer frontend, then the front wheel.

Zach and Matt show up to help and everyone takes a section. Matt and Zach were on the oil tank and fender.

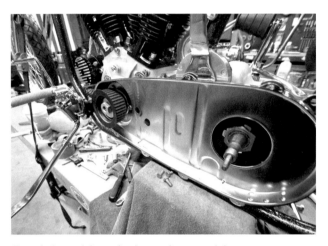

Daniel and I took the primary drive.

We decide to whack another three inches off the ends of the bars: perfect!

In the meantime, Daniel had finished installing the BDL inch and a half belt drive and buttoned up the primary. It's a classic look with no mess.

Here is a nice trick for locating a p-pad. Sharpen two bolts at the bottom of the seat pan, . . .

. . . throw some blue tape down on the fender and once you get it in place, tap it and it will leave indicator marks that tell you where to drill.

The tape protects the paint as you drill as well.

Using a set of hollow punches, I made some leather washers to mount the fuel tank.

Our SU manifold stuck out about three inches too far so Daniel went to work with the TIG. Great look man!

Lowbrow hooked us up with these bad-ass cloth spark plug wires. It goes real well with the old style tuna can coil.

With that, some oil and brake lines had to be figured out; the pipes went on and we were almost done.

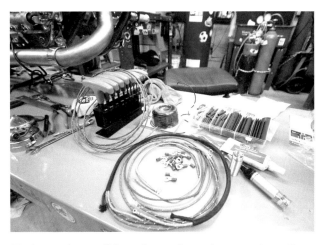

To keep it traditional, we found some lengths of cloth wiring to use to make our harness.

In the end, this was the exact bike that I wanted to build. Thanks to all my brothers who showed up and helped me get it done like this!

16
PAUL'S ADVANCED CUSTOM BUILD

My dad picked up a 1949 EL Pan/Shovel for a decent price. There were some really cool parts on the rolling basket case we got, but the bike was a complete bucket. We took it back to the shop and almost immediately started tearing into it.

The frame was an original H-D wishbone that had been cut mercilessly; it was cut at the sidecar loops and turned into a straight leg with about 6" of stretch. We initially wanted to take the frame back to original specs with some replacement forgings. Instead, pop sourced a decent wishbone frame for a fair price.

So the plan is to build a traditional Panhead chopper; the kind with no stretch or rake, with one of our Super Narrow Springers, old style running gear, mag fired, plus a few other goodies: light and tight. We sent the engine down to Craig at D&C Cycle in Eureka, MO for a complete rebuild. We were pleased to find out that the bottom end was actually all S&S, and quite bigger than the stock 61" displacement the ELs sported. I sourced a nice Panhead topend for it, and D&C laced up a bulletproof motor that will prove to be a real ass-hauler.

Dad snatched from me a beautiful Morris Magneto that I had set aside for my chop-off project, and an SU carb was pried out of the hands of buddies Chuck and Leon over at Jammer Joint Motorcycles. Considering all of the mix-matched pieces going into this build, we decided to call it Hobo Stew.

As you can see, the bike was pretty whacked. The geometry is pretty cool for a chop, but the work is scary to say the least.

The one we will be working with is only missing a few pieces from its original trim, like the tool box bracket, and some smaller things. Upon closer inspection, we found some of the tabs and brackets needed a little tidying up.

The first thing that stuck out was the bar behind the seat area. We replaced this with a new piece.

A minor fix that needed attention was the caterpillar sized repair weld in the rear fender mount behind the trans.

It's amazing how much better things look when you take a few minutes to do them the right way.

The brake crossover tube on our frame had been cut for some reason. We will be running a later model juice drum so it wasn't a major concern, but I wanted to bring this frame back - close to original shape.

You can see the difference in dimension on this stock frame.

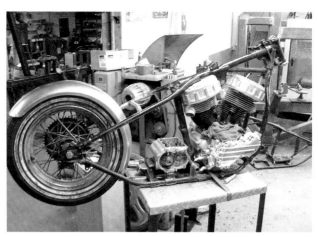

After a little frame cleanup, we decided to mock-up the bike a little to get the feel for what it's going to look like. Looks good to us.

We used a piece of 1 inch DOM tubing, spun down to the needed length. We turned down a piece of brass so the O.D. with the I.D. of the tubing, to keep the tubing aligned.

I always start at the back and work forward. To do this, we always align the drivetrain first. To align motor and trans, pass bolts thru all of the mounts, and lightly tighten all fasteners.

Then I welded the two tubes, pulled the brass bar, and ground down the welds.

Once you have your engine and tranny on the same plane, you may need to shim the front pulley out to make them dead even. You can find these shims at any reputable shop.

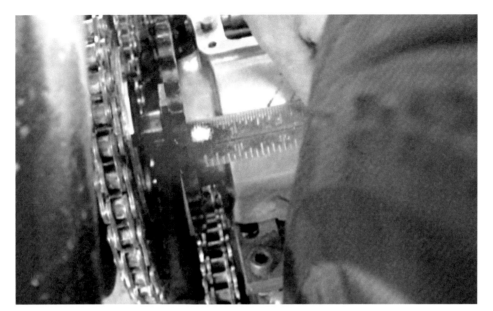

With our motor and transmission aligned, we moved to the rear wheel. I use a laser and stick it up to the sprocket on the rear wheel with the wheel all the way forward in the axle slots. Using a small square, I measured the difference between the front and rear.

Here I am marking where I want to trim our Bare Knuckle ribbed fender down. Instead of trimming the back, I get the back set where I want it, and then trim the excess from the front/bottom.

After marking the edge with a marker, I pull a straight line with some masking tape.

And with a cutoff wheel, I lose the extra inches.

To make the corners smooth, I grab a piece of round stock and lay out a radius with marker. Then I grind accordingly.

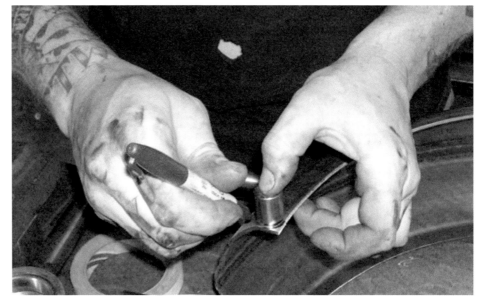

To provide ample space between the tire and fender, I laid some chain on the tire. Normally this would sit a little high for my liking, but the raised rib section in the middle of this fender makes the surrounding fender sit lower.

Using clamps and a piece of flat stock, we are able to keep the bottom of the fender flush with the bottom of the frame rails.

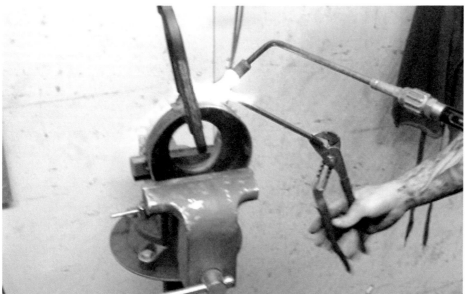

To make my fender mounts I picked out some ¼" x 1" flat stock. The radius of the fender is the same as a four speed clutch shell, so I clamped one end to the shell and heated it up. Remember when I told you that oxy/fuel rig would come in handy?

I ground material away from the center section of my mount to allow room for the fender rib.

After fabbing a similar piece for the frame tab and drilling and tapping holes, I tacked and welded the entire mount.

I did something similar to the bottom mount, only instead of two pieces of flat stock, the mount is via round stock that is drilled and tapped. It bolts on from under the stock mount.

For the grab bar, I am using the stock tabs on the top side of the axle castings, along with some ¾" round stock that is drilled and shouldered for a 5/16-18 Allen bolt. After bending the ½" grab bar around a fire extinguisher, and a little fish mouth, I start tacking.

On the fender I use the same mounts as described in our Mounts chapter.

Since these bars are not going to be adjustable, I had dad hop up on the bike and get in a comfortable position, and we marked where the bars would best fit him.

We decided to make the ape hangers real narrow at the bottom, and gradually widen at the top. The only problem this presents is that normal risers will not work.

Instead of running a traditional bar mounted master cylinder, we are going to use an early style cable lever and a remote master cylinder.

Using my level and a tape measure, I mapped out where I would make each bend.

Again, since all of this will be permanent, I had my dad put his hand where it would comfortably operate the brake.

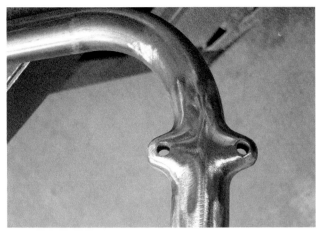

As opposed to leaving the weld raw, I opted to fill the area in around the spud, giving it a more "molded" look. I used a small carbide burr and belt sander to smooth out the area.

I hit the welds with a 2" Scotch-Brite disc and the welds were gone. I went ahead and made the welds around the risers disappear as well.

I waited to fill the backside hole in so I could run a tap through all the way. With all of the extra welding it is a good idea to clean up the threads.

Further mocked-up; ready for tanks. For this bike we wanted a set of fatbob tanks, but we decided to make our own out of aluminum.

A quick filler weld and the holes are gone.

I traced the general shape onto a manila folder and then transferred that to some 16 ga. 3003 aluminum sheet. I cut it with the plasma cutter and ground off the rough edges.

Annealing brings the material back to a dead-soft condition. Which allows you to better work the metal. This is a process that slowly brings the temperature up to 800 degrees.

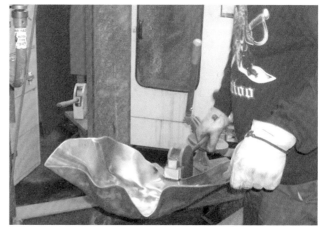

As the center of the piece is stretched, it begins to wrinkle. I use a Mittler Brothers' shrinker to relieve some of the wrinkling.

Here's the annealed sheet with the buck.

You can see the hammer dents and the shrinking marks at this point.

Time to stretch. I use a large bag about 80% full of steel bird shot and a large Fournier plastic hammer and start by hammering area that needs the greatest amount of stretching.

To remove the "walnuts," I use the Mittler Brothers' planishing hammer. A pneumatic hammer in a frame, with an anvil that the hammer strikes.

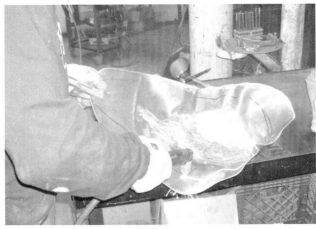

After a good bit of shaping, you can see that a lot of material can be removed. The plasma cutter makes quick work of removing metal.

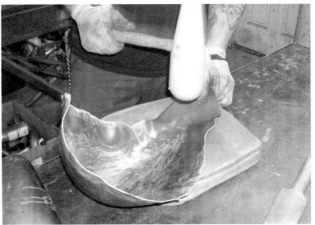

Now I begin to hammer the rear section of the tank. You will learn that sheetmetal fab is a game of patience. You cannot work on one section to completion and then move to the next. Every strike on the panel affects every little section of the work piece.

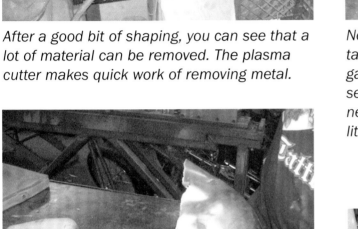

There are still some large wrinkles, even after trimming. I use a t-dolly and a large wooden slapper wrapped in leather to evenly hammer the wrinkles down.

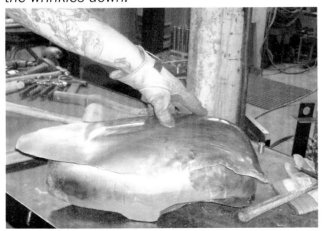

Here I'm checking progress by comparing the shape to my buck.

Using a flat anvil in the English wheel, I roll some of the wrinkles out.

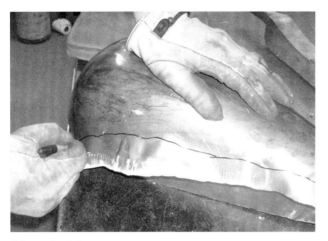

More to trim.

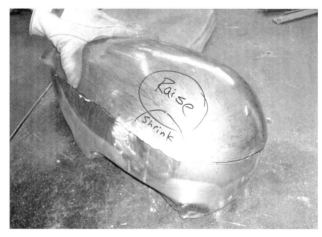

Here is the main reason you use a buck. Your eye may not tell you that there are high or low spots, but the buck will. I take a Sharpie and make notes to myself where work is needed.

The tank side is starting to take shape.

I try to use hand tools, it is easy to go too far with power tools. In this instance the small area calls for precise strikes, and the planishing hammer provides just that.

Back to the slapper and t-dolly.

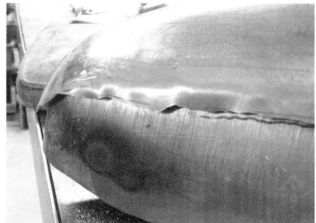

That's better.

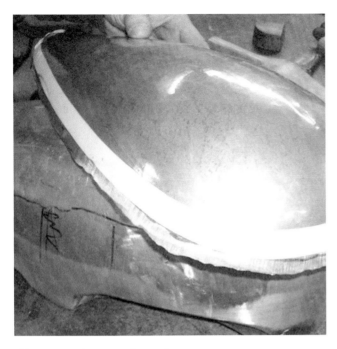

Time to trim one last time.

The next step is to make a pattern for the latter top and front sides.

I lay out the cardboard on another piece of annealed aluminum and transfer the pattern. Using the same techniques as earlier, I made the panel, and then he tacked it in place. You can see that the rear needs one last piece.

After welding your panels together, be sure to clean up the welds on the inside as well as the outside. If not, you will not be able to dolly out the imperfections. I like to leave a little bit of the weld and use the planishing hammer to smooth out the rest.

Since the frame we are using is a pretty cherry original, I didn't want to remove any tank mounts, but I also wanted to rubber mount the tanks. I made a couple of tabs that use the stock mounts, and provide rubber mounting.

The right side inner panel is already shaped. You can see as I weld the left side on, that it is quite larger than the right side.

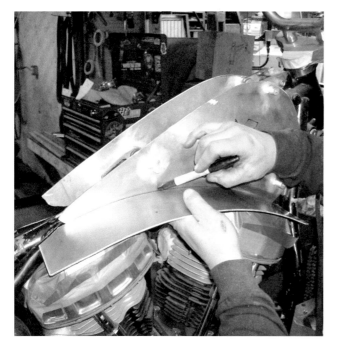

I taped a chunk of ¼" aluminum to the top of the rocker boxes to allow sufficient room between the engine and the bottom of the tanks. I traced the general shape of the bottom panel. After this, it is removed and cut to size.

This test fit shows you the basic shape the bottom will have. This part is a trial in patience. A lot of taking the tank off and putting it back on. The right side is by far the hardest, as you have the rocker covers to work around.

After a ton of fitting, you can see that we have a few areas where material needs to be added, as well as a few where aluminum needs to be trimmed.

After employing the same principles as on the right side tank, I clamped the left side together.

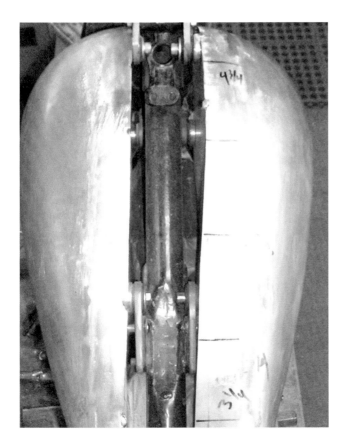

Here are both sides tacked to the inner panels. You can see a few things in this pic; you can see that the gap in the middle is different from side to side. You can also see the hash marks and measurements on the right side that helped us match one side to the other when fitting the two to the inner panels.

Here is a stock set on my bone stock '64. You can see that even factory tanks had major irregularities from side to side. We will be running a stock dash panel and a leather trim cover but I still want the rear half to look like stock.

With another piece of manila folder and a Sharpie, I traced the inside edges of my stock tanks. This leaves a nice impression in the folder.

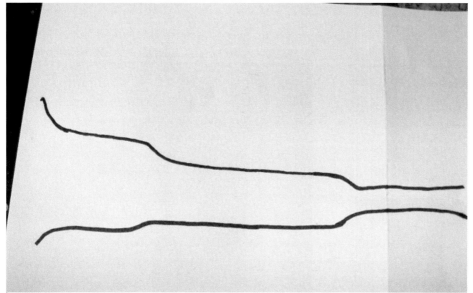

Here is the pattern after I traced it with a marker.

Using the same technique, I traced the area between the panels on the new tanks. Then I transferred that pattern to the aluminum sheet and cut it with the plasma cutter.

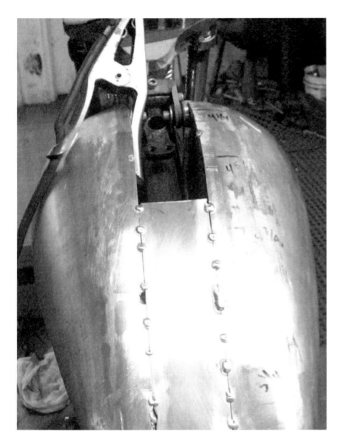

Paying close attention to keeping everything straight and even, I tacked the panel to both sides of the tanks.

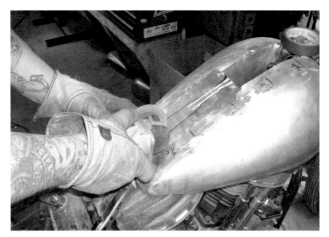

These are the little details that go a long way in my opinion. You have to go slow here though, one slip and I'm in big trouble.

A little work with the carbide burr...

After finding the centerline of the frame and marking it on the panel, I used our pattern from the stock tanks to mark my cut lines.

...and the tanks done!!

Of course there is still a lot more to go, but at this point we're down to the trimmings. From here, some parts go out to paint, some go out for chrome and some final touches get added to come up with our finished product of Hobo Stew.

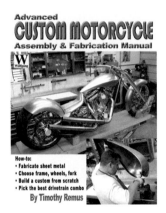

ADVANCED CUSTOM MOTORCYCLE ASSEMBLY AND FABRICATION

It all started in the mid-90s when a few people decided to build their own bike from aftermarket parts. Today, every small town has a Custom bike shop, and every motorhead wants to build a sexy softtail like the ones they see on TV.

Wolfgang Publications and Tim Remus were there at the very beginning, and they're back with Advanced Custom Motorcycle Assembly & Fabrication. Part catalog, part service manual, and part inspiration, this new book offers help with planning the project, getting the right look, fabricating parts and assembling that custom bike you've been dreaming about.

Three start-to-finish sequences, with builders like Donnie Smith and Dave Perewitz, show not just how the best bikes are bolted together, but how the unique one-off gas tanks are shaped and then fitted to the stretched soft-tail frames.

| Nine Chapters | 144 Pages | $27.95 | Over 400 color images - 100% color |

SHEET METAL BIBLE

Sheet Metal Bible is a compendium of sheet metal fabrication projects, everything from simple shaping operations to multi-piece creations like fenders and motorcycle gas tanks. Each of these operations is photographed in detail. Meaty captions help the reader to understand what's really happening as a flat sheet of steel slowly morphs into the convex side of a gas tank.

While some of the craftsmen work with hand tools, others prefer the English Wheel. The book is filled with work by legendary fabricators like Ron Covell, Craig Naff, Rob Roehl and Bruce Terry. Projects include components for two and four-wheeled hot rods. Each metal has its place in the metal shop, and this new book includes tips on how to work with, and weld, both metals.

| Ten Chapters | 176 Pages | $29.95 | Over 400 photos, 100% color |

PRO PINSTRIPE TECHNIQUES

In more than forty years of pinstriping and creating signs, there isn't much that East Coast Artie hasn't done. With Pro Pinstripe Artie shares everything he's leaned during his long career. Find out first hand why Artie chose a particular color combination, or a certain brand of paint for a particular job.

To illustrate how pinstriping works in the real world, the bulk of this new book is made up of 12 start-to-finish pinstriping sequences performed by Artie and a small cadre of guest artists. Each of the guest artists, from Nub, (Of Orange County Choppers fame), to Mr. J, Mikey Fredrick, Howie Nisgor, and Zeke Lamanski, have their own style, and their own contribution to this extensive pinstriping book.

| Eleven Chapters | 144 Pages | $27.95 | Over 400 photos, 100% color |

HOW TO BUILD AN OLD SKOOL BOBBER

Kevin Baas begins the second edition of his How to Build an Old Skool Bobber book with a little history, the history of bike building at home, as seen through the eyes of a young man watching his Vietnam-Vet father build a chopper at home in 1970. In his father's eyes, and Kevin's as well, the engine and frame should to be old skool - and genuine Harley-Davidson if possible - but the rest can and should come from swap meets, or the sweat of your own two hands. Kevin lays out the basics of bike building, starting first with the ideal components: which engine, which frame, and the differences in the various years. Next, things to watch out for when buying old parts, and how to fix the parts you do buy. Additional chapters describe brake systems, both early and late, tires and wheels, and frame geometry. Four complete start-to-finish bike assemblies round out this hands-on book.

| Thirteen Chapters | 144 Pages | $27.95 | Over 500 photos, 100% color |

Wolfgang Publication Titles

For a current list visit our website at www.wolfpub.com

ILLUSTRATED HISTORY
Sturgis 70th Anniversary	$27.95

BIKER BASICS
Custom Bike Building Basics	$24.95
Sheet Metal Fabrication	$27.95

COMPOSITE GARAGE
Composite Materials Handbook #1	$27.95
Composite Materials Handbook #2	$27.95

HOT ROD BASICS
Hot Rod Wiring	$27.95
How to Chop Tops	$24.95

MOTORCYCLE RESTORATION SERIES
Triumph Restoration - Unit 650cc	$29.95
Triumph MC Restoration Pre-Unit	$29.95
Harley-Davidson Panhead Restoration	$34.95

SHEET METAL
Advanced Sheet Metal Fabrication	$27.95
Ultimate Sheet Metal Fabrication	$24.95
Sheet Metal Bible	$29.95

CUSTOM BUILDER SERIES
How to Build an Old Skool Bobber Second Edition	$27.95
How To Build The Ultimate V-Twin Motorcycle	$24.95
Advanced Custom Motorcycle Assembly & Fabrication	$27.95
Advanced Custom Motorcycle Chassis	$27.95
How to Build a Cheap Chopper	$27.95
How to Build a Chopper	$27.95

AIR SKOOL SKILLS
Airbrush Bible	$29.95

PAINT EXPERT
Kosmoski's New Kustom Painting Secrets	$27.95
Advanced Custom Motorcycle Painting	$27.95
Advanced Custom Painting Techniques	$27.95
Kustom Painting Secrets	$19.95
Pro Pinstripe Techniques	$27.95

TATTOO U Series
Into The Skin	$34.95
Tattoo Sketch Book	$32.95
American Tattoos	$27.95
Body Painting	$27.95
Tattoo - From Idea to Ink	$27.95
Tattoos Behind the Needle	$27.95
Advanced Tattoo Art	$27.95
Tattoo Bible Book One	$27.95
Tattoo Bible Book Two	$27.95

NOTEWORTHY
Guitar Building Basics Acoustic Assembly at Home	$27.95

Sources

Bakerstown Radiator
1620 Middle Road Ext
Gibsonia, PA 15044-7989
(724) 443-8855
www.bakerstownradiator.com

Bare Knuckle Choppers
21 Highway A
Hawk Point, MO 63349
636.338.4355(p)
www.bareknucklechoppers.com

Buchanan's Spoke & Rim, Inc.
805 W. Eighth Street
Azusa, California 91702
www.buchananspokes.net

CP Cylinder Head & Machine
8340 Lillian Hwy.
Pensacola, FL 32506
850-607-7880

Cycle Warehouse
200 S Main St
Butler, PA 16001
(724) 282-7278
www.cyclewarehouseonline.com

DLK Performance & Machine Shop
PO Box 1
Russellton, PA 15076-0001
(724) 265-1020

Eastwood
263 Shoemaker Road
Pottstown, PA 19464
(610) 323-2200
www.eastwood.com

Ed Fish Machine
2627 Butler Logan Rd
Tarentum, PA 15084
(724) 224-0992

Fabricator Kevin
44306 Macomb Industrial Drive
Clinton Township, Mi 48036
www.fabkevin.com

Gardner-Westcott Company
10110 Six Mile Road
Northville, Michigan 48167
(248) 305-5100
www.gardner-westcott.com

Greco Gas, Inc.
450 Grantham St.
Tarentum, PA 15084
724-226-3800

Handy Industries
401 South 2nd Avenue
Marshalltown, Iowa 50158
855-752-5446
www.handyindustries.com

Indian Larry Motorcycles
400 Union Ave.
Brooklyn, NY 11211
(718) 609-9184
www.indianlarry.com

Lincoln Electric
22801 St. Clair Ave.
Cleveland, OH 44117
216-481-8100
www.lincolnelectric.com

Lowbrow Customs
Ohio
440-479-8129
www.lowbrowcustoms.com

M. Arman Publishing
PO Box 785
Oak Hill, FL 32759
Telephone: (386) 673-5576
www.arman-publishing.com/

Metco Steel Warehouse
81 Kiski Avenue,
Leechburg, PA 15656
(724) 842-3151

MSC Industrial Direct Co
75 Maxess Road
Melville, New York 11747-3151
1-800-645-7270
www1.mscdirect.com

Metzeler
www.metzelermoto.com

Papa Clutch Customs
3110 Hwy 92
Ainsworth IA 52201
319-657-2220
www.papaclutchcustoms.com

Paughco, Inc.
30 Cowee Drive
Carson City, NV 89706-7734
800-423-2621
www.paughco.com

Relic Custom Stripes
Austin Minnesota
(507) 438-8725
www.relicstripes.com

Slingin' Ink
809 5th Ave.
Grinnell, IA 50112
641.236.9800
www.slinginink.com

Spectro Oils
93 Federal Rd.
Brookfield, CT. 06804
Phone: 203-775-1291

Speedking USA
5970 Dry Ridge Road
Cincinnati OH, 45252
513-885-7433
speedkingphoto.com

Twisted Choppers
27085 S Tallgrass Ave.
Sioux Falls, SD
605.498.0105
www.twistedchoppers.com

Willie's Tropical Tattoo
825 South Yonge Street
Ormond Beach, FL 32174-7633
(386) 672-1888
www.tropicaltattoo.com